Beech Mountain Breeze

By
Ed Robinson

Copyright © 2019 by Ed Robinson

All rights reserved. No part of this work shall be reproduced in any manner without the written permission of the publisher.
Published by Leap of Faith Publications.

This is a work of fiction. Any actual person or place mentioned is used fictitiously. Though some of my work is based on my real life experiences, most of it is a product of my imagination.

For my grandson Jaxen, who was the first of us to cross the swinging bridge atop Grandfather Mountain on a cold and windy day. May life provide him with many more adventures.

Beech Mountain

At an elevation of 5506 feet, Beech Mountain is the highest incorporated town east of the Rockies. The town has a full-time population of 350, but the population swells to 10,000 at the peak of ski season in the winter, and 5,000 during the summer.

Even though there are only 350 permanent residents, there are over 2,350 dwelling units on the mountain. Beech Mountain is a popular location for vacation and second homes for many people from North Carolina to Florida.

Lance Armstrong, who survived a bout of testicular cancer, was out of shape and considering retirement in the spring of 1998. In a final effort, coach Chris Carmichael brought him to the mountain for a week of riding. Armstrong says he regained his competitive edge when he reached the top of Beech Mountain one morning during that trip.

Carmichael brought Armstrong to Beech in part because of the rider's previous success there. In the mid-1990s, when the Tour Du Pont passed through this range, its most famous stage finished atop the mountain. Armstrong won the stage in 1995 and finished first or second in each year from 1993 to 1996.

The mountain's biggest attraction is the Beech Mountain Ski Resort, which provides world-class slopes and an unending menu of special events to visitors year-round.

BEECH MOUNTAIN — A malfunctioning gate release valve at Buckeye Reservoir has led to the emergency rescue of a diver as well as a state of emergency and mandated water rationing for Beech Mountain citizens, according to a notice sent by the town on Wednesday.

"We're looking at a time table of a minimum of 24-72 hours," said Beech Mountain Town Manager Tim Holloman, referring to the duration of the water restrictions.

Under stage five of water conservation, which is the most severe restriction, "only the minimum use of water is permitted." Holloman estimates that the advisory affects 1,500-2,000 people.

"Your cooperation in this water emergency is crucial in helping the town address this water shortage," Beech Mountain Town Clerk Tamara Mercer said in a statement. "The town cannot fully express that requesting this voluntary citizenry participation is of utmost importance. All conservation efforts include: No usage of washing machines or dishwashers. No flushing toilets when not necessary. Using bottled water for drinking. No showering."

Holloman said that water distribution to the citizens of Beech Mountain will take place on Thursday from 8 a.m.

to 4 p.m. at Beech Mountain Volunteer Fire Department Station #2, located at 513 St. Andrews Road.

The water restrictions do not affect Beech Mountain Resort, which has a separate water system, the town stated.

The restrictions come after an incident on Nov. 19, when the town and a private contractor began the process of cleaning, maintenance, and assembly of the gate release valve. A diver attempting to close the gate release valve had to be rescued Nov. 20 after his leg became caught in the device, according to a statement from the town of Beech Mountain.

"He was under water for three to four hours," Holloman said.

Shortly after 10 p.m., divers from Carter County Tennessee Water Rescue successfully rescued the diver, and he was transported to Watauga Medical Center, Holloman said. The diver was in good condition as of Wednesday morning, according to the statement.

"He talked to us this morning and said 'thank you,'" Holloman said of the diver.

"The town of Beech Mountain gratefully thanks all those who helped carry out a successful rescue operation," according to the town's statement. "Because of the malfunction of the valve, the town is deeply involved in stopping the loss of water from the reservoir."

Responders from various agencies worked together to aid the rescue including: Avery Sheriff's Office, Avery EMS, Avery Emergency Management, Beech Mountain Police Department, Beech Mountain Volunteer Fire Department, Beech Mountain Utilities, Carter County Tennessee Water Rescue, Carolina Water Department, Elk Park VFD, Linville VFD, Linville Central Rescue, Red Cross and Watauga Emergency Management.

Holloman said that a new dive team will come in Thursday to cap the valve, which will allow the reservoir to fill back up and the restrictions to be lifted. A permanent fix will come at a later date.

"We won't release (the restrictions) until the water level rises," Holloman said.

The town's notice says that a statement will be released immediately upon being able to lift the restrictions.

Call Beech Mountain Police at (828) 387-2342 or Beech Mountain Town Hall at (828) 387-4236 for further information.

This story is developing, check *www.wataugademocrat.com* for updates.

How I Go to the Woods

Ordinarily I go to the woods alone, with not a single friend, for they are all smilers and talkers and therefore unsuitable.

I don't really want to be witnessed talking to the catbirds or hugging the old black oak tree. I have my way of praying, as you no doubt have yours.

Besides, when I am alone, I can become invisible. I can sit on the top of a dune as motionless as an uprise of weeds, until the foxes run by unconcerned. I can hear the almost unhearable sound of the roses singing.

***

If you have ever gone to the woods with me, I must love you very much.

Mary Oliver

One

Brody and I heard about the draining of Buckeye Lake and thought it would be an interesting thing to see. We drove up the Beech Mountain Parkway to satisfy our curiosity. Several dozen onlookers were already at the lake. We left our car at a small park that we'd visited previously and walked to the water's edge.

Most of the people there were content to view the empty lake from shore, but a few were out mucking through what was usually under six feet of water. I had no interest in sinking my shoes in the soft mire until I heard a woman scream. She started waving her hands in the air and yelling for help. Brody and I looked around at our fellow observers, none of whom had any interest in helping. We tightened our shoelaces and began the arduous slog out to the woman in need.

She'd discovered a body. It was that of a teenage girl. The lack of decomposition meant she hadn't been dead long. She probably hadn't floated yet, as sometimes it takes several days for that to happen. If she'd been floating, someone would have spotted her before now.

"Can you call 911?" I asked the woman. "We don't have a phone."

"I can't get a signal up here," she said. "I would have called them already."

"Do you want to stay with the body while we go get help?"

"I'd rather not," she said. "I'll go."

"The police will want to talk to you," I said. "You found her first.

"I'll go to the police station," she said. "Easier than trying to find a signal."

"Don't alert the folks on shore," I suggested. "We don't need a bunch of people walking all over the place."

She agreed and left to find a cop. Brody and I stood there looking at the victim. She'd been a pretty young girl with her whole life in front of her. That future was now gone. I was tempted to examine her for signs of foul play, but decided it was best not to touch her. I'd leave that to the cops, or medical examiner. I put my hands in my pockets and stepped a little further from the body.

"I can hear the gears turning in your head," Brody said. "What are you thinking?"

"That this isn't the crime scene," I said. "Assuming it was a murder."

"If it were suicide there would be some visible sign," she said. "A rope, slit wrists maybe."

"She could have overdosed," I said. "Swallowed a bunch of pills and walked out into the lake."

"It's so sad," she said. "Either way it's tragic."

"If there is any evidence to be found it's on dry land," I said. "The lake isn't that big. Wouldn't take long to canvas the shoreline."

"We've got to wait here for the police," she said.

"We can poke around some after they get here," I said.

"If they allow it," she said. "They might call this whole area a potential crime scene."

"Or they might ask for volunteers to search for evidence."

"Stay within their expectations," she said. "If they say no we'll just walk away."

"Killjoy."

The town of Beech Mountain had their own police department. I'd never dealt with them, so I had no opinion as to their competence. I did know that the murder rate on this mountain was zero. Crimes of any kind were almost non-existent, outside of the occasional break-in of a vacant house. We'd seen some of their officers hanging out at the ski resort, acting as security. I didn't have high hopes that we'd meet an expert investigator.

An officer arrived within twenty minutes and confirmed my suspicions. He didn't know what to do. I suggested calling the State Police in to help with the investigation.

"Let me call the Chief," he said. "I've never even seen a dead person before."

He used his portable radio to call for help. His chief agreed that they needed outside assistance. He was told to stand by and to keep the public away from the scene. Brody and I were part of the public. He asked that we go to shore and wait until more officers arrived. He was sure that someone would want a statement from us.

We trudged back through the mud to the park. Our shoes were nearly ruined. We took them off and tried to rinse them off in a puddle that the receding water had left behind. It was a useless exercise. It was thirty minutes before a State Trooper pulled into the parking area. I recognized the man immediately. He'd been on a team that I'd led to a fugitive on my mountain. He often worked with my cop friend, Rominger.

"How's it going, Johnson?" I asked.

"Fancy meeting you here," he said. "Why is it that you always show up when there's a dead body?

"We didn't find the girl," I said. "We just came to see what an empty lake looked like."

"First impression of the scene?"

"Nothing visible," I said. "I didn't touch anything. Can't say how she got there, unless she swam on her own."

"Drowning?"

"Maybe," I said. "Maybe not. Can you check her for signs of injury?"

"I can," he said. "But it looks like it's going to be a mess. Getting her out of here won't be pleasant either."

"Need some help?"

"I appreciate the offer," he said. "But I better call for more hands and some boots."

"Mind if we sniff around the park?"

"I'm not giving you permission," he said. "But suit yourself."

"If someone starts yelling at me I'll tell them you forbid me," I offered.

"Wait until after I examine her," he said. "Might give us something more to work with."

Johnson went out on the lake to meet up with the Beech Mountain cop. Brody and I sat on a picnic table and watched. Some of the bystanders came over to ask us what was going on.

"Dead girl in the mud out there," I said. "That's all I know so far."

That was enough for them to start spreading the word. Within minutes everyone at the park knew there was a body on the bottom of the lake. Every single person pulled out their smartphones, trying to check into Facebook or text a friend, in spite of the poor cell coverage. Some took pictures, even though they couldn't make out what was going on from where they stood.

"If you want to go sniffing around in the woods, you should take me home first," Brody said. "Bring Red back up here if you want."

Red was a hound mix that we'd found walking along Pigeon Roost Road. After failing to locate his owner, we made him a member of our family. He was an excellent tracker. So far he and I had assisted local law enforcement twice. We found a lost little girl in less than one hour on our first mission. We also located two missing teens who'd survived a bear attack near Crab Orchard Falls.

The combination of his nose and my ability to become one with the woods made us a formidable team. I wasn't sure how he could help in this situation, though.

We had nothing to go on. Red needed a scent to follow. I doubted the dead girl's body would provide it after being in the lake for a day or two, but my dog would enjoy a romp through some new territory.

"Okay," I said. "I'll run you home and pick up Red."

Brody didn't have much interest in sharing my exploits in the woods or on the mountain. She was fine with a mild hike to see a waterfall, but extended walks on a mountainside weren't her cup of tea. She'd rather sit in our warm cabin reading a book or baking cookies. If I didn't enjoy hiking, she'd have me fatter than Santa.

Red was ready and willing to get out of the house. I let him run around the yard and do his thing before loading him into the car. I drove back to Buckeye Lake to find cars and trucks from every police department within twenty miles. An ambulance from the Banner Elk Fire Department was on site as well. The crowd of onlookers had increased dramatically in size.

Johnson and the Beech Mountain cop were covered in mud. The girl's body was on a gurney, covered with a sheet. The officers from the various agencies huddled together discussing the situation, struggling to come up with a plan. I nodded at Johnson, pointed at Red first, then at the woods.

"Hold up a minute, Breeze," he said. "I want you to meet someone."

I walked over to them, feeling uncomfortable around so many cops, until I saw the pretty girl cop.

"This is Angelina Will," Johnson said. "She's got some real investigative experience and even some forensic skills. Do you mind if she tags along with you?"

Angelina wasn't just pretty, she was sexy, even in a police uniform. She was petite but curvy, with brown hair and eyes. I hadn't been taken aback by a woman's beauty since the day I'd met Brody. Her smiled revealed perfect white teeth. We shook hands, and I felt an electric sensation run through me. I was surprised at my reaction and tried to stay cool. This was a possible murder investigation. I couldn't let my attraction to her interfere with my search for clues, nor my relationship with Brody. Still, her presence made me feel a bit more alive.

"Johnson tells me you have special skills," she said.

"I've got a way with the woods," I told her. "Just comes naturally."

"Well, I've got a way with a crime scene," she responded. "We should make a good team."

"So I'm officially part of this search?" I asked Johnson.

"You volunteered to help us find clues," he said. "You and your dog. I didn't think you'd mind teaming up with Angelina for the day."

"Of course not," I said. "My pleasure."

Miss Will and I broke off from the main group and moved to a picnic table in the park to develop a strategy. I saw that she wasn't wearing a wedding ring. Sometimes I was too aware for my own good. I noticed that she was wearing perfume. It smelled nice but seemed strange for a cop on duty. She was not wearing any makeup, but she didn't need any. She moved and spoke in a coquettish manner, flirting with her eyes and mannerisms. Maybe I imagined these things, but she was hard to resist. I tried to steer the conversation to the matter at hand.

"The natural water flow tells us that she started floating near here," I said. "Otherwise she would have ended up at the dam. If we can find out what time the lake was fully drained, we could recreate her journey to the point she was found."

"If there was water in the lake, we could float something and make a good guess at what time she entered the water."

"I understand that's going to take a few days," I said. "They have to fix a gate valve first."

"At least we can rule out all the shoreline between where she was found and the dam," she said.

"Half the lake ruled out," I said. "Unless her killer moved her a good ways before dumping her in the water."

"Doesn't seem likely," she offered. "But we can't rule out suicide either. What if she dosed up and wandered around before entering the lake?"

"Okay, so half the lake is not ruled out," I said. "But we can prioritize our search area. I say we start right here and work our way towards the dam."

"Where's the dog come in?" she asked.

"I'm not sure yet," I said. "But if we get a scent on something curious, he'll follow it wherever it leads."

"Might come in handy," she said. "What's his name?"

"Red," I said. "Red, this is Angelina."

She knelt down and scratched behind his ears just the way he liked it. He licked her face and tried to give her his paw.

"He's a handsome one," she said. "Just like his father."

I could feel my cheeks turning red, and I was embarrassed to be so obviously affected by her charms. I was a hard man. I'd been through a lot of dangerous situations in my life. I was competent and capable in almost any situation, but I'd never been able to resist the magnetism of a beautiful woman. It was my Achille's heel. I'd done some really stupid shit on behalf of pretty girls in my life. Now was not the time for a repeat performance.

"We've got work to do," I said. "Follow Red and pay attention. If he or I see something worth investigating, I'll let you know."

"I like a man that takes charge," she said. "Lead the way."

I did not imagine her flirtation. It may have been real. I wasn't a bad looking guy after all. On the other hand, it may be her way of controlling the situation or even controlling men. It wouldn't be the first time a woman used her looks to her advantage. She could use me to solve this crime, then take all the credit. I'd be a useful idiot, spurred on by her feminine guile. I could live with that. She was nice to be around either way.

We entered the woods at the shoreline and started wandering about. I figured that whatever went down had to have happened close to the water. I concentrated on a twenty-foot swath, working back and forth, taking everything in. Red did the same. He didn't know what he was looking for, but he knew we were after something. Angelina stayed behind us, keeping quiet. Whenever I looked back at her, she gave me a sweet smile. It was all just a walk in the park.

What we needed was more information. Have they found evidence of foul play? Is there an indication of the cause of death? Who is she? We were on a snipe hunt with nothing to go on. Normally, I would take every available piece of data and roll it all around in my head until I hit on a likely solution. I wasn't in a position to solicit more information from law enforcement, but Angelina was.

I stopped and sat on a log, waiting for her to join me. She sat too close to me, giving me a fresh whiff of her perfume. Her shoulder touched mine, and she gave me a little nudge.

"This could be romantic under different circumstances," she said.

"A romp in the woods with a complete stranger?"

"Depends on what you mean by romp," she said. "I suppose there are too many prying eyes in the woods today. What are we supposed to be looking for anyway?"

"Your guess is as good as mine," I replied. "Why don't you call someone and ask for any new details. Anything that will help us."

"Such as?"

"Who the kid is," I said. "Was she local? Reported missing? Any obvious wounds? History of drug abuse? They've got to know something by now."

"Got it."

She stood and paced about while she talked on the radio. The only thing they'd found was a deep gash on the back of the victim's head. There was obvious blunt force trauma. They had not identified the victim. No teenage girls were reported missing. They would update us as new information became available.
"Someone whacked her on the head," she said. "That's all we know, so far."
"Not a suicide," I said.
"Nope, we've got a murderer on Beech Mountain."

We continued zig-zagging along the shoreline. The further we got from the park, the thicker the brush became. Red didn't seem to mind, but the waist-high weeds were a pain in the ass. Angelina walked in my wake as I knocked them down. It made for tough going, but it turned out to be a blessing. Red hit on something in a small area where the weeds had already been knocked down.

It was a man-sized depression in the undergrowth, bolstered by additional sticks and grass piled around the edges. My dog was all over it with his nose. He circled

around it then looked at me. He gave me one quick bark. He was smelling something or someone.
"What do you think he's found?" Angelina asked.
"Looks like someone bedded down here," I said. "Made themselves a comfy pallet and blocked the wind."
"Can your dog track him from here?"
"As soon as I say go," I said.
"Let's get after him."
"Find him, boy," I told Red. "Sniff him out. Let's go."

The dog circled two more times before finding which way the mystery man went. He wanted to run, but I had to reign him in. We couldn't run after him through the thicket, but it was clear he had the scent. I increased my pace just a little, and Angelina soon fell behind.
"Wait up, mountain man," she said.
I tugged at Red's leash to slow him down. He protested but obeyed my command. My partner caught up, and we continued to follow his nose. We soon came upon a second area of interest. It was less obvious than the first, but Red was certain. Under the low branches of a big pine, the needles had been piled up to form primitive bedding. There was no other sign of man, no trash or personal items stashed away. We would never have discovered it without the dog.

I let him sniff it over until he was satisfied. He wasn't sure which way to go, which indicated to me that the man had been here more than once, coming and going from different directions. Red would go with the freshest scent, so I waited for him to decide. It gave us a chance to catch our breath.

"What do you think we have here?" asked Angelina.

"A vagrant living in the woods," I said. "Not necessarily our killer."

"Not until we find more clues," she said. "But who could live out here? I thought the homeless would avoid the mountains. Tough way to go. No services, no heat, no help."

"You'd be surprised," I said. "I once befriended an old codger who'd been living on my mountain for years. Long story."

"I'd like to hear it sometime," she said.

"Maybe someday," I said. "Red's ready to go. You good?"

"Good to go," she said.

The woods got even thicker from there. Even Red was having a difficult time making headway. Our mystery man had made no trails or left any trace that he'd been this way, but Red was insistent. He led us back to the water's edge and stopped. He looked confused. Had the man entered the water here? I took him back inland

and had him circle the general area. He gave no sign of picking the scent back up. Our trail was gone.

"What do we do now?" Miss Will asked.

"We can either stumble around blindly trying to pick up his trail again, or we can go home and regroup."

"I for one vote we call it a day," she said. "I wasn't prepared for cross-country mountain hiking. We need some water at the very least."

"I agree," I said. "This is going to take more time and effort than I was ready for."

"Maybe they've learned more about the girl," she said. "Let's head back to the park."

Red was disappointed. He didn't like not being rewarded for finding his target, but continuing to search that day was not a great idea. We'd given it our best shot. We'd learned something. Whether it was relevant to the girl's death remained to be seen.

Two

Back at the park, we reported to Johnson. He seemed to have taken control of the command post. We told him what we'd found. Another team had searched the opposite side of the lake and come up empty. No one had covered the area around the dam, but workers were still there repairing the gate valve. It didn't seem like a killer would want to be too close to that much activity. For all we knew, the killer could be a thousand miles away by now. Maybe Angelina and I had been chasing a bum who lived in the woods, nothing more.

"I don't think there's much more we can do here today," said Johnson. "Running out of daylight."

"Will you be back out here tomorrow?" I asked.

"Probably," he said. "Maybe we'll get some more information from the Medical Examiner. Maybe the girl's parents will hear about this. A lot can happen overnight. Are you willing to come back tomorrow?"

"I've got nothing better to do," I said.

"I'll be here too," Angelina said. "Breeze and I are good together. I'd be happy to assist."

Johnson gave me the look. He knew about Brody and seemed to question Angelina's motive to stay close to me. I gave him a shrug and walked to a bench and sat down. I was soon joined by my new female friend.
"He seems to think we've got something going on," I said. "You do know that I'm spoken for?"
"I gathered," she said. "Doesn't mean we can't work together. Whatever happens as a result, I can't say."

It was the moment in time when I should have drawn the line. All I had to do was tell her that I was in love with Brody, that I'd never cheat on her, and that nothing was going to happen between us. I didn't do that. It wasn't the first time in my life that I knew my decision was wrong, but did it anyway. I had a long history of that. Going against what I knew was proper, had been the reason for most of the grief I'd encountered. I told myself that it didn't mean I would sleep with Angelina, necessarily. We were simply sharing a little male and female attraction. No harm done.

She seemed to sense that we'd crossed some imaginary line. She'd pulled me over it, and I let her. It was not a full surrender, but she'd won the first skirmish. I should have gone home immediately. Instead, I stayed and talked for a few more minutes. I was finding it hard to pull myself away.

"How did you become a cop?" I asked. "What made you decide?"

"I was a big fan of strong woman characters on the TV shows," she said. "Marg Helgenberger on CSI. Mariska Hargitay on SVU. Gillian Anderson in X-Files. I wanted to be like them."

"Avery County ain't exactly New York City," I said.

"Real life ain't TV," she said. "There are still a lot of barriers for women in the real world of law enforcement."

"I've had some experience with the good old boy network in these parts," I said. "You'd be better off in a more progressive area if that's what you really want."

"This is my home," she said. "I tried to get hired in Asheville, but no go."

"So you settled for a deputy position with Avery County," I said. "You must be the hottest deputy to ever wear the badge, Miss Will."

"I think my looks hurt more than they help," she said. "I wouldn't mind being Sheriff someday, though."

"Your picture will look great on campaign signs," I said. "I'd vote for you."

"Thanks for being so sweet."

The conversation had gone far enough. I was playing with fire, and I knew it, but I couldn't help myself. This woman flipped all of my switches. She was hot, smart and capable, just like Brody. I had to get out of there.

"Look," I said. "I've got to go home. Red wants his dinner and Brody is waiting for me. I'll see you tomorrow, okay?"

"Sure, partner," she said. "It's been nice getting to know you."

"Likewise," I said over my shoulder. I was already walking to my car.

I wallowed in guilt on the ride home. I was way out of line allowing things to progress so far with Angelina. I absolutely adored Brody. She was my life and reason for living. Why had I been so foolish? Miss Will had a magnetism that I had a hard time resisting, but Brody and I had a lifelong commitment. I would not betray that, no matter how hot Angelina was. When I got home, I relayed the events of the day, leaving out the fact that my cop partner was a beautiful woman. Red lay in front of the fire, twitching and dreaming about hunting down our mystery man.

After dinner, and after a shower, I took Brody to bed and used my sexual frustration to please her to the fullest. I held her tight afterward, confirming to myself that I was committed to her, always. I'd find the moral strength to resist Miss Will, knowing that if I didn't, I'd lose Brody forever. I couldn't let that happen. I almost confessed to my attraction for the lady cop, but I couldn't bring myself to do it. Nothing was going to happen, so Brody didn't need to know.

There was a much smaller crowd at the lake the next morning. Johnson had sent whatever officers he could spare to knock on doors and interview folks that lived near the lake. There weren't many houses nearby, and many of them were seasonal. Two deputies from the Watauga County Sheriff's Department were already working on the opposite side of the lake. Johnson was talking with Angelina when I arrived with Red.

"The victim is still a Jane Doe," said Johnson. "We've got no ID on her. The word is out over a three-state area. We circulated a photo after cleaning her up as best we could. The ME says the blow to the head didn't kill her. COD is drowning."

"Did you bring those deputies up to speed on what we found yesterday?" I asked.

"I told them," he said. "They said they didn't see anything similar, but they were looking for more obvious clues. They don't have a dog either."

"When do they plan to start refilling the lake?" I asked.

"Later today," he said. "If there is anything useful out there in the mud, it will be under water tonight."

"You going out there?" I asked.

"I've got my waders in the truck," he said. "I'm not hopeful, but it will be my last chance before any evidence gets flooded."

"I'd shoot for finding the weapon," I said. "The perp wouldn't know that the lake would get drained. Good chance he tossed it into the water."

"My thoughts exactly," he said. "You sure you don't want a job?"

"Positive," I said. "That would never fly anyway, and you know it."

"Just wish some of my coworkers were as sharp as you," he said. "It would make my job a lot easier."

"I haven't met too many people as sharp as Breeze," Angelina said. "He's got a real aptitude for this kind of work."

"He's been a great help to us more than once," Johnson said. "Adding that dog to the team has worked out well too."

"Don't expect any miracles this time around," I said. "We have zero clues except for a dead girl and the fact that somebody had been sleeping in the woods nearby. It's practically a Bigfoot hunt."

"If you find the guy, have Will detain him for questioning," he said. "Call me right away."

"I'm going to venture further away from shore today," I said. "I'm concentrating on the mountain man rather than the girl. It's all we have to go on."

"Sounds good," he said. "If I get any new information I'll let you know."

I led Red and Angelina over a wooden walking bridge and onto a hiking trail that rose upward from the park. I took note of the high-quality hiking boots that my partner wore. She had a backpack with water and snacks as well. She wore a wide-brimmed hat to keep the sun off her face and a bandana around her neck. She could have been a model for L.L. Bean.

"At least we're better prepared today," I said.

"I hope I don't look too frumpy for you," she responded.

"I'm sure you'd make anything look good," I said. "But let's try to stick to business, if you don't mind."

"We won't find any clues on this trail," she suggested. "Too frequently traveled."

"You're right," I said. "I doubt he would set up camp so close to the park either. I want to get up a little higher, then veer off into the bush."

"Should we split up?"

"That's a strategy worth considering," I said. "But we can't get too far apart. We've got no way to communicate with each other."

"We use the trail as a centerline," she suggested. "You and Red go down towards the lake. I'll go the other way. We backtrack and meet on the trail. If I find anything curious, we'll take the dog to it. Keep going back and forth like that until we hit on something good or run out of daylight."

"Okay, but here's the deal," I said. "If there is a person of interest roaming these woods, it would be best not to announce our presence. Do you think you can move with enough stealth that he doesn't know you're there?"

"You mean sneak around the woods?" she asked.

"Move like smoke," I said. "Make no sound. Make yourself invisible as best you can."

"Is that it?"

"Not exactly," I said. "You sure you want to hear how I do it?"

"Positive," she said. "You are the master, and I am your student."

"Promise not to laugh," I said. "But it works for me."

"I'm ready to learn," she said.

"Use your ears to listen as you've never listened before," I said. "Use your nose to smell every detail of the woods. Be aware, then increase your awareness. Take in all the sights, sounds, and scents that you can. I mean really amplify your senses. I call it mountain Zen."

"Zen and the Art of Mountain Hiking," she said. "I think you've got a book title there."

"It takes a little practice," I said. "And you've got to be open to it. Sort of let yourself get into it."

"This is how you track people?"

"It was my sole method before I got Red," I told her. "I've managed to outwit experienced woodsmen that way. They move, they smell, they make a sound, and I'm on them."

"I think I understand the general idea," she said. "Putting it into practice is something else entirely."

I sat down on the ground and raised my hand to hers. She took it and sat beside me. I lowered my voice to a whisper.

"Take some slow, deep breaths," I said. "Calm yourself. Make your heart to slow down."

"Like target practice."

"Yes," I said. "Now listen. Listen for sounds that you normally ignore. Hear the rustling of the leaves, songs of the birds, traffic far away."

"I'll try."

"Now smell the dirt and the trees," I said. "Smell my aftershave, Red's breath, the new leather of your boots."

"I can smell all of them," she said. "I'm trying to turn up the sounds."

"Stay calm and let it come to you. Don't close your eyes. You need to see everything at the same time."

"It's so much all at once," she said. "How do you sort through it?"

"Single out the stimulus," I said. "First it smells like woods. Break it down into each individual scent. It's tree bark, mountain laurel, rhododendron, worms in the dirt, mud in the lake."

"I think I understand," she said. "The sound is all one buzz at first. Then it's the creek, the breeze, the leaves, and the grass. I can hear cars in the village."

"You're a natural," I said. "Now the trick is to move like smoke while remaining in the Zen state."

"Walk, chew gum, and practice extra-sensory perception all at the same time."

"That's all there is to it," I said.

"You've mastered this?" she asked.

"When I'm not distracted by a beautiful woman," I said. "So we should split up, allow each of us to work undisturbed."

"But keep regrouping on the trail, right?"

"Yes, but maintain sound discipline as best we can," I said. "We'll exchange info in whispers, then move on again."

"I've got it," she said. "I'm ready if you are."

Red and I slid down the hill towards the lake. Having him hindered me somewhat. I couldn't move as silently or as fluidly as I would like, but his nose would be the superior talent if we did find anything. I kept him moving slowly with his head up to catch any scents on the wind. We stopped every twenty yards to listen to our surroundings. Angelina was not making any noise that we I could hear, but her perfume was still in my nose and on my mind.

When we reached the shoreline, I let Red sniff around in either direction until he was satisfied that there was nothing of interest. We climbed back up the hill as quietly as we'd come down. I waited on the trail for Angelina to return. She shook her head no.

"Me neither," I whispered. "You take the lakeside this time."

We moved along the trail another fifty yards before breaking off in opposite directions. She was doing an excellent job of moving with stealth. It was good to see that she'd taken my instructions seriously, even though we were looking for the tiniest needle in the biggest haystack. We repeated this procedure another dozen times before deciding to take a break. She pulled out two bottles of water and some trail mix. We sat on a fallen tree and mulled over our options.

"We found those two spots yesterday," she said. "Both were on the lakeside of the trail. Maybe we ought to concentrate there."

"Either one of us could have walked by another spot today," I said. "Just didn't see it."

"It does seem like an impossible task," she said. "We're like two blind people hoping we trip over something."

"I'm not discouraged yet," I said. "If there's someone living out here, someone who may have killed the girl, we'll find him eventually. What worries me is the possibility that he's not here anymore. We can find his hideouts, but it won't do us any good if we don't find him."

"Even then," she said. "He might not be our killer."

"It's all we've got," I said. "At least for now. Anytime you want to give up just let me know. I won't hold it against you."

"I won't quit until you do," she said. "Maybe not even then."

Now she'd really endeared herself to me. She had much more spirit than I'd originally thought. She wanted to learn from me, and she wanted to solve this crime. For the first time since we'd met, I felt like we could work together without letting the mutual attraction interfere. Red approved of her as well. Whenever we stopped, he sat with her and freely accepted her affection. Neither of us would ever tell Brody.

It was late afternoon before we came upon something of interest. I found the slightest remains of a campground on the lakeside of the trail. Most people wouldn't have noticed a thing. The first indication that caught my eye were rub marks on a branch. I pictured a tarp having been tied there. Beneath those marks, the grass was flattened down. Between a grouping of small rocks, I found the remnants of a tiny fire after I brushed the leaves away. Red was sniffing all over the site. There was no doubt that someone had slept here, probably more than once. It was much more of an encampment than the first two spots we'd discovered, at least in my mind's eye. The clues were very subtle and well-covered. This man did not want to be found.

I brought Angelina to our find after we met on the trail. Red was anxious to go to work, but I couldn't leave her behind. I put a finger to my mouth and pointed out each detail. She nodded that she understood, so I urged Red to do his thing. He once again had the man's scent. We followed him for a few hundred yards before he stopped. I had seen no signs along the way, no footprints, no broken branches, nothing that would tell me a man had passed this way. We only had Red's nose to guide us, and now he was stumped.

We all came to a stop, and the woods got real quiet. I looked all around me. The man didn't get beamed up by a starship. How did he eliminate his trail? How could his scent have stopped here? I eyed the rocks that were high enough to reach low-hanging branches. He could have only gone up. Great, I thought to myself. We're chasing Tarzan. The canopy above us was thick but not endless. He would've had to come down somewhere nearby. Red didn't have his trail, but he could pick up his scent again if I got him on it.

"Come on, boy," I said. "Circle around. Sniff him out."

Three

My hound dog started a sweep of the area, desperately trying to pick up the scent again. While he worked, Angelina and I spread out looking for any type of clue. So far I hadn't even noticed a footprint. We were far off the trail, and the vegetation was much too dense for hikers. I looked for weeds or grass that had been stomped down or freshly broken branches on the smaller bushes.

The sky got a little darker making our search more difficult. Depending on where you are on a particular mountain, the sun can disappear as early as four in the afternoon. We were running out of time. Red kept getting farther and farther away, so I gave up and moved closer to where he was searching. I waved for Angelina to follow. We couldn't stay out here too much longer.
"If he doesn't get on the scent soon we'll have to pack it in," I said. "I'd like to get back to the park before dark."

"Okay if I check in with Johnson?" she asked.
"If someone is out here, they already know we're here too," I said.

Johnson told her that he had some additional information. The other search team had quit for the day, and he was ready to go home as well. He asked that we return to the park. I reluctantly agreed. Before heading back, I impaled a granola bar wrapper on a sharp thorn to mark the spot. I called Red back, and he looked as reluctant as I was. He didn't like these fruitless searches.

We kept up a fast pace on the return trip. Angelina didn't lag behind or complain. We'd moved past our underlying attraction and stuck strictly to business all day until we slowed to cross the wooden walking bridge.
"You are one sexy mountain man, Breeze," she said. "It's been a pleasure walking behind you and watching you work."
"My turn to walk behind you tomorrow," I said. "Turnabout is fair play."
"I don't have a problem with that," she said. "I'll have to wear tighter pants, although they'll be harder to take off."
"You'll be keeping your pants on, missy," I said.
"You never know when the moment will strike," she said. "A girl has to be prepared."

We stepped off the bridge and saw Johnson waiting impatiently at his truck. Our banter stopped before he was within earshot. He seemed irritated that we'd made him wait.

"The girl came from a rental cabin here on the mountain," he said. "The family is French. They speak poor English and have no internet or cell phone reception up here."

"Why didn't they report her missing sooner?" Angelina asked.

"It's not the first time she didn't come home at night," he said. "When she failed to show up a second night they realized something was wrong."

"How old was she?"

"Fifteen," he said. "Seems Europeans have more progressive ideas about teenagers out partying all night."

"Is there a nighttime party scene up here?" I asked.

"She's wasn't old enough to get into bars," he said. "But the ski resort stays up pretty late. Everyone is on vacation, having a good time. They think she found some kids her age to hang out with."

"How many people are at the resort right now?" I asked.

"Couple hundred, at least," he said. "Not as many as during peak ski season, but it's still hopping."

"Why would another kid whack her on the head?" I asked.

"Rape?" asked Angelina.

"Medical Examiner says no sign of rape," said Johnson. "No recent sexual activity was detected, consensual or otherwise."

"Are you working to identify any of these teens that she might have been hanging out with?" I asked.

"Beech Mountain boys are doing their best," he said. "They know the resort better than we do and their presence doesn't upset the clientele."

"What else have you learned?" I asked. "If anything."

"This mountain has a history of break-ins of unattended homes," he said. "Never anything valuable stolen. Some don't go reported for months until the owners return. Some don't even report anything taken, just that the place had been broken into."

"That would be consistent with the ghost we've been looking for in the woods," I said. "He could be nice and cozy in some empty cabin as we speak."

"We're not that far from the ski village," he said. "Three or four miles. Plenty of houses between here and there."

"If you don't mind I'd like to make a suggestion," Angelina said.

"I'm all ears," said Johnson. "That's why you're on this case."

"We need a map of the mountain," she said. "With all the roads marked and house numbers. I'm sure the Beech Mountain PD has something that would work, if not we create one using Google Maps. We stick a pin at each of the alleged break-ins. A few more pins at the spots Breeze and I discovered. See if we can't triangulate this guy's working territory. Narrow our search."

"Might take a while to put together," Johnson said.

"We've got time," she said. "It's a murder investigation. No one is going to ask us to quit, especially not the girl's family."

"I'm sure the resort would be happy to see the man caught," I said. "What's the buzz there?"

"I really don't know," he admitted. "I'll ask the Beech boys."

"I always liked their music," I said, trying to lighten up the mood. "Help me Rhonda, help, help me, Rhonda."

Angelina elbowed me in the side. Johnson didn't seem to see the humor in it either. I guess police work is serious business, no joking allowed.

"I think she's got a good idea," Johnson said. "Breeze?"

"You guys are the cops," I said. "But it seems like a good start to me."

"Okay, let's wrap this up for tonight," he said. "I'll get with the Beech Mountain Chief and work on our map.

Let's meet at their station in the morning, say around ten."

"I'll bring the donuts," Angelina said.

"I'll leave Red at home," I said. "He can't read maps."

We broke up our little huddle and Angelina and I moved towards our cars. We paused next to her driver's door and watched Johnson drive away. I turned back to her and suddenly found her lips on mine. In theory, I didn't want her to kiss me. In reality, I didn't want her to stop. A little devil appeared on my left shoulder.

"This is it," the devil said. "Go for it."

A little angel appeared on my right shoulder.

"I've got one word for you, buddy," the angel said. "Brody."

The angel was right, as he always was. I would follow his advice; it just took a full minute to make up my mind. Her lips were soft and sweet. Her perfume was intoxicating. I felt the smooth skin of her cheek and neck. I put a hand on the back of her neck and pulled her towards me ever so slightly, just enough pressure for her to feel it. Then I put that same hand on her chest and gently pushed her away. I'd come dangerously close to her breast.

"We've got to stop," I said. "I've got to get home."

"It's okay," she said. "That was just a taste."

I didn't respond because I was tongue-tied. Rarely was I at a loss for words, but she'd taken me by surprise. I hadn't resisted as I should have. I felt a little weak in the knees. I turned my back to her and walked away while I still could. I told myself that I loved Brody all the way home. I remembered all of her wonderful attributes and all that we'd shared. I could see her sparkling eyes in my mind.

I let Red cruise the back yard and take care of his business before going inside. I grabbed a beer to wash the taste of Angelina off my lips. I took a shot of whiskey to wash her memory out of mind.

"You okay," Brody asked. "A beer and a shot before even saying hello?"

"Hi, baby," I said. "Long day. Dead girl and such. Cops. Not much progress."

"You'll figure it out," she said. "I have faith in you."

"We're putting together a better plan in the morning," I said. "They're making a map of known break-ins up there. We're working on the theory that the man I've been trying to find is the same man who's entering vacant homes."

"How is he tied to the girl's death?"

"He's not, necessarily," I said. "But it's all we've got."

"Seems pretty thin," she said.

"They think the girl hooked up with some other kids at the ski resort," I told her. "They're asking around now, trying to make some connections, but that's real police work. All I can do to help is try to find the guy in the woods. That's why I'm still included."

"So you've been blindly walking around in the woods the past few days by yourself?"

"First of all, I don't do anything blindly," I said. "I'm doing my thing as best I can. I've found some clues. Second, they've teamed me up with an Avery County Sheriff's Deputy. She can apprehend the suspect if and when we find him."

"She?"

"Yes, she," I said. "Deputy Angelina Will. Reasonably competent. Doesn't bitch. Follows my lead."

"Is she pretty?"

"Very much so," I said. "Rather stunning actually, but you've got no worries."

"Why not?"

"Because I'm hopelessly in love with you and have been for quite some time," I said. "You know that I'd never do anything to screw that up."

"I trust you," she said. "But it's good that you told me you're working with a hottie."

"Trying to be honest," I said. "No point in hiding it from you."

"How old is she?"

"Younger than us," I said. "Low forties maybe."

"Not married?"

"I didn't ask, but she doesn't wear a ring," I said.

"Young forties, pretty, but not married," she said. "Must have issues. Probably a psycho."

"I'm guessing her career choice may have something to do with that."

"Why?" she asked. "What guy doesn't want to marry a hot cop? You're with me, aren't you? I was a cop, and pretty hot if I say so myself."

"You have an excellent point; I must admit," I said. "But I'm not your average guy. I wasn't afraid to be with a strong-willed and gorgeous woman. Most guys are intimidated by that."

"The looks or the strong will?"

"Both," I said. "Trust me on that."

She mulled that over for a few seconds before conceding my rebuttal. I knew that she knew there was more to my story than I'd let on. She didn't push it, though, she let it drop. God bless her. She'd given me her trust with a silent warning not to betray it. I knew it was time to keep my mouth shut and not belabor the situation. I could only talk myself further into a hole. Neither of us said another word about my working relationship with the pretty policewoman.

Four

I met Johnson, Angelina, and the Beech Mountain Chief the next morning as scheduled. Red was a little miffed that I didn't take him with me. I stopped on my way out the door to get a kiss from Brody. She ground her hips into mine and held the kiss a little longer than usual. I took it as a message that I had a sexy woman right here at home, so there was no need to think about anyone else. It worked well until I got my first look at Angelina passing out donuts. She had indeed worn tighter pants, and she'd failed to secure the top few buttons of her blouse. She smiled at me with the face of an angel.

"Good morning, folks," I said. "Any progress on a map?"

"I had a big paper one printed earlier this morning," said the Chief. "We still need to pin the locations of the reported break-ins. I've got the list of addresses right here."

"I've got Google Maps fired up," said Johnson. "None of us knows all the little side streets, especially the more remote ones."

"How many houses are we looking at?" I asked.

"Thirty in the last year," the Chief said. "If we go back five years there's over a hundred."

"Thirty break-ins in a year and no suspect?" I asked.

"No one has ever seen the guy," he responded. "Remember, these places are all vacant a good part of the year. They might not discover the breach for many months. There are likely more entries that have never been reported, like those that leave a key hidden somewhere they think is clever."

"So we have a homeless perp wandering around looking for opportunities for shelter," I said. "Maybe a meal or a new pair of socks. But other than that he's harmless."

"That's why there's been no urgency to catch him," Johnson said. "We're aware, but it's become sort of a legend around here. The Beech Mountain Hermit. He's done no real harm."

"So why would he suddenly decide to kill?" I asked. "A murder of a pretty young girl is sure to bring the heat down on him."

"I have a theory," Angelina said.

"Shoot," said Johnson.

"She caught him in the act," she said. "Got a clear look at him and would be able to identify him."

"Let's explore that idea," Johnson said. "Pin the house the girl was staying in first."

The Chief gave him the address, and he put a pin on the map just off Pinnacle Ridge Road. The location was halfway between the ski resort and the Buckeye Lake.

"Breeze, can you guess the locations that you found in the woods near the park?" Johnson asked.

I put three pins in the approximate locations in the woods. They were on the opposite side of the lake from the girl's cabin, but a large community center was on the closest side. The lake was small, and the walk around to the other side was a short one. There were no houses in the immediate area.

"I'm not sure what this tells us," said the Chief. "Let's start pinning the rest of the addresses."

In less than an hour, we had thirty more pins on the map. The pattern had developed well before we were finished. Pinnacle Ridge Road was the backbone of the target area. The pins were isolated between Buckeye Creek, which ran into the lake, and Grassy Gap Creek, which ran out of the lake, and up into the more developed area on either side of Pinnacle Ridge. There were no reports near the Golf Course or the ski resort. There were no reports in the town proper. He'd stayed away from the more populated areas, hitting only the more remote houses where there were no street lights or close neighbors.

The farthest pins to the west, the ones I'd found in the woods, were quite close to the Tennessee border. The lands beyond that were undeveloped. There was a lot of mountain territory, providing a hermit with an unlimited number of places to hide.

"His real home is somewhere to the west," I speculated. "He comes down to the lake and uses one of his temporary shelters, then finds an empty house. Hangs out a few days, finds some food, maybe he takes a shower. Then he retreats to his permanent shelter."

"Somewhere along the Tennessee border," said Johnson. "No way we can locate him out there."

"After his encounter with the girl he's going to hang low for a while," said Angelina. "He can't risk another break-in so soon afterward. He will know that we're looking for him."

"The weather is getting warmer too," I said. "As long as he has a way to get food he'll stay away."

"So we don't have shit," said the Chief. "What are we supposed to do now?"

No one had an answer. We could make a reasonable assumption about what had happened in this case, but we had no idea how to catch the culprit. We all grabbed another cup of coffee and a donut. I stared at the map, willing a clue to present itself. The man was anonymous, and a ghost in the woods. I wasn't willing to sit and wait for him to strike again, but that seemed like our only option.

"The girl's family is going to return to France soon," said the Chief. "I dread telling them that we've got nothing."

"It sucks," Johnson said. "But these mountains aren't like the streets of Paris. We may never catch this guy."

"I can't justify using the man hours to fumble around hoping for a miracle," the Chief responded. "I think we're looking at an open case for a long time. An unsolved murder on Beech Mountain won't sit well with the Chamber of Commerce."

"I'm the only one from the State Police left on the case," Johnson said. "Without something to go on, I doubt I'll be back up here."

"I might be able to talk the Sheriff into a few more days," said Angelina. "But I don't see where it will do much good."

We were defeated, which stuck in my craw. I wasn't ready to give up, but I couldn't articulate a reason to continue. The only saving grace I could see was Angelina leaving my life. The temptation had become hard for me to ignore. If we called it quits on this case, I could cross that problem off my list.

"We are all making an informed decision based on the resources available and the lack of information we need to catch this guy," I said. "Let me continue on my own. No one has to pay me. I'll scour those woods on the other side of the lake and try to track the man back to his permanent shelter, on my own time."

"What happens if you find him?" Johnson asked. "We've been down this road before."

"He's not a shooter as far as we know," I said. "I'll make a citizen's arrest if there is such a thing these days. I'll hold him for you."

"How will you communicate with us?" he asked.

"You could lend me one of those radios," I suggested. "Knowing that it won't be turned on unless I need to call you. This would be my operation solely. You can sweep up when I'm done."

"Do you think you have any chance to find this guy?"

"Not a good one," I admitted. "Might be impossible, but maybe I'll get lucky. Won't cost you anything. Nothing lost."

"I'm inclined to allow it," Johnson said. "Chief?"

"What can it hurt?" he answered.

"I'd like to be a part of it," Angelina said. "But I doubt I can get approval. I'm probably out of this going forward."

"No offense, Miss Will," I said. "But this is the type of work I do alone."

"I know," she said. "Mountain Zen. I get it. I was starting to feel it up there with you the other day. Maybe we can arrange further training sometime."

"Brody wouldn't approve," I said. "But it's been a real treat getting to know you."

"You don't know the half of it," she said, handing me her business card. "Keep me in mind."

She leaned in to kiss my cheek, taking my hand in the process. She looked deep into my eyes without speaking a word.

"I'll see you around, Breeze," she said. "Nice to meet you too."

She grabbed the last donut and walked out of the Chief's office. I couldn't help but watch her walk. Her tight ass almost hypnotized me before she got into her car. I was equal parts happy and sad to see her go, but I now had one less complication in my life.

"Have you tapped that?" asked Johnson.

"No, I have not," I said. "And don't let any rumors get started. Not that I wasn't tempted."

"You've got more willpower than me," he said. "Sweet ass."

"For the record," I said. "She offered, but I declined."

"I don't know that I could have done the same," he said. "I mean I love my wife and all, but damn."

"It wasn't an easy decision, but I'm glad I didn't," I said. "I'm quite happy with what I have."

"As you should be," said the Chief. "Enough of the locker room talk. I've got to tell some important folks that we've gotten nowhere with this case. It won't be a pleasant chore."

"Tell them that you've arranged for a consultant to continue the investigation, pro bono," I said. "Make it sound more important than it really is."

"I'll see if I can work that in," he said. "You'll keep me apprised of your progress?"

"Absolutely," I said. "If there's anything to report."

Johnson and I went outside and stood in the parking lot. I thought that he wanted to push me on my relationship with Angelina Will, but he was more concerned with our failed investigation.

"Do you think you can get something done out there in the wilderness?" he asked. "I don't think I get the mountain Zen thing."

"I don't have high hopes, to be honest with you," I said. "But I'm in love with these mountains. I thrive in these woods. If there's anyone alive around here that can find this guy, it's me."

"And you're willing to do this for us free of charge?" he asked. "Just to give you a reason to wander around the hills."

"Something like that," I said. "Not much to do at my place. Making love to Brody only takes a few minutes out of my day. The rest is just eating and sleeping."

"You've got the life," he said. "The rest of us envy you. How do you afford it?"

"Long story," I said. "Not all of it good. Let's just say I'm making amends now by helping you guys. Balancing the scales and whatnot."

"I'll take it," he said. "Rominger needs me back in Boone. I don't see us getting anywhere on this case. We'd close it all together if you weren't involved."

"No promises," I said. "It's a real longshot."

I tried to formulate a plan as I drove back to the cabin. Brody would be happy to hear that my working relationship with the pretty female cop had ended. She might not be so thrilled with my offer to work for free, even though we didn't need the money. On the other hand, she knew that I needed something to occupy myself. It would be no different than hiking on our own stretch of land. I didn't foresee any danger in it.

I figured that I'd take Red back to where we'd lost the man's scent. I'd let him ramble around some more, and if he couldn't find anything, we'd look elsewhere. If we somehow managed to get close, I'd leave Red at home and go full stealth mode to get close to my target. He would never expect that someone could find him. He'd be off guard, and I could close in on him undetected. That was the best case scenario. The worst case would be me wandering around blind in unfamiliar territory and finding nothing.

I needed more to go on, but additional clues weren't available. Maybe something would come to me after a good night's sleep. Angelina had fogged my mind somewhat. Putting some distance between us might kick start the old noggin. I'd talked it over with Brody after I got home.
"Some unknown person who lives in the wilderness comes into Beech Mountain and breaks into unoccupied homes," she said. "He's been doing it for years. There's

no uproar because he doesn't steal anything of much value and hasn't hurt anyone. Am I with you so far?"

"That's our theory," I said.

"Then suddenly he decides to kill a teenage girl because she busted him?" she asked. "Why would he do that?"

"Maybe he didn't mean to kill her," I suggested. "He wanted to bonk her on the head and escape."

"If that were the case, he wouldn't have dumped her in the lake," she countered. "He would have left her where she fell."

"Maybe she wandered around in a daze and fell into the water," I offered. "The blow to the head didn't kill her. Drowning did."

"That's a few too many maybes," she said. "What if the Beech Mountain hermit whacked her? What if she fell into the lake on her own? What if he dumped her body? Your working theory is full of holes. It's barely a guess."

"That's why I'm running it by you," I said. "The smartest investigator I know."

"Think they'll put me on the payroll?"

"I'm not even getting paid at this point," I said. "They know I'm tilting at windmills."

"But they've got nothing to work with," she said. "What happened with the interviews at the ski resort? Did they find anyone who knew the girl, or remembered seeing her?"

"I don't know," I said. "I never heard."
"Can we get our hands on the map you were working on?" she asked.
"Didn't think of it," I said. "Good idea."
"We need to lay the groundwork before you go off chasing ghosts," she said. "I'll go with you to see the Beech Mountain Chief tomorrow. Let's get as much information out of him as we can."
"It's a start," I said. "Thanks, by the way."
"Just trying to contribute."

That night I snuggled with Brody in bed longer than usual. We didn't make love, I just held her close and told her that I loved her. I stroked her hair and hugged her tightly. She was the greatest gift I'd ever received in life, and I wanted her to know it. I didn't think of Angelina Will, only the beautiful angel lying next to me.

The next morning after breakfast, we went to the Beech Mountain Police Department. The Chief was studying the map and scratching his chin.
"Good morning," I said. "This is my gal, Brody. She used to be with the FBI."
"I've been brought up to speed on you two," he said. "I think I'm glad to have your help on this."

"You are welcome to sever our relationship at any time," I told him. "If we make you nervous."

"The state cops vouch for you," he said. "I'll have to take their word for it. This department isn't exactly full of detectives. We wouldn't even be here if it weren't for the ski resort. Glorified security guards is what we are."

"We'd like to hear about those interviews your men did," I said. "What did they find?"

"She was at the lodge that night earlier," he said. "She was the fifth wheel with two young couples from out of town."

"Are those kids still here on the mountain?"

"Nope," he said. "But we have their parent's contact information."

"What's their story?" I asked. "Did she leave with someone? Was she drinking or doing drugs?"

"The kids swear they didn't have any booze," he said. "But I'm not sure I believe them. None of them are of age."

"Smoking a little weed maybe?"

"All four denied it," he said. "There was a band playing that night. They hung out by the fire listening to music. Eventually, the girl disappeared. They don't remember what time that was. They don't know how she was supposed to get home."

"So all we know is that she was there, at the resort," I said. "She left and got herself killed."

"And her body ended up in the lake a few miles away," he said. "Dead girls don't walk that far."

"We don't know where the attack occurred, so we've got no crime scene," Brody said.

"Have any of these houses reported a break-in more than once?" I asked.

"No, they have not," he said. "So if the girl saw the man, it would be at a house that's not pinned on this map, but what was she doing there?"

"Maybe she didn't go straight home," Brody said. "She met a boy, and he was taking her back to his place."

"His parents would be there," I said. "Maybe it wasn't a teenager. Maybe it was a young man with access to a house up here."

"Now we're creating scenarios," Brody said. "Plus how would we ever figure out the house where it took place?"

"Any ideas, Chief?" I asked.

"The incident area is fairly well-defined," he said. "No condos, no high-density areas. We could narrow it down to a hundred homes or less. Rule out the full-timers and knock it down some more."

"So we need to search the grounds of seventy or eighty places," I said. "Look for blood or blunt instruments."

"Too much for my meager resources," he said. "But knock yourselves out."

"At ten addresses per day, we'll be done in a week," Brody said. "We just need to know where to look."

"Let me get Officer Sally in here," he said. "He knows what's what as far as the locals go. Born and raised up here."

Brody and I looked over the map while we waited. We'd only driven down Pinnacle Ridge Road twice before the girl was found. It was hard to take in the scenery while driving because the road was so winding. The homes were scattered about the wooded areas. Some couldn't be seen from the road. I thought we should prioritize those. Brody agreed.

When Officer Sally arrived, we told him what we were looking for. We wanted a list of homes that were mostly unoccupied but had not reported a break-in, within the target area.

"I understand," he said. "I'll cross reference with Google Maps and try to narrow it down some. Give me a few hours, at least."

"Don't bust your balls," I said. "We'll come back tomorrow and start working on the list that you create."

"That would be great," he said. "Feels like real police work for a change. Give me a day, and I'll have a good list for you."

"Thanks, man," I said. "See you tomorrow."

The Chief got on the phone to find someone to fill in for Sally. He seemed relieved to turn over the investigation to two total strangers that weren't affiliated with law enforcement, which I found odd. There were originally three county Sheriff's departments, the town department, and the State Police involved. Now it was down to Brody and me. Real cops had deemed the investigation hopeless. They had better things to do than waste their time on a lost cause. The only clue was the dead girl. A murder was a black mark on the community, but it could be kept quiet as not to discourage tourism. If we wanted to volunteer our services for free, they were all happy to accept. It probably made them feel better about wiping their hands of it.

Brody and I stopped at Bodegas for some shrimp tacos and a beer. It was becoming one of our favorite restaurants in town. Stonewalls was higher-end, but it was too expensive to frequent.

"You knew more about investigating a crime than the Chief did," I said.

"I've been involved in more than a few murder investigations," she said. "He hasn't."

"Now we put our shoes to the street for some old fashioned detective work," I said. "You up for this?"

"It's how I found you," she said. "The best technology that the FBI had to utilize couldn't do it, but I did."

"And the rest is history, as they say."

"It will be fun to be out in the field with you," she said. "In civilization, not in the boonies."

"House to house," I said. "Looking for clues."

"Million to one chance we find anything," she said. "He could have whacked her down by the lake. We don't know where she went after she left the resort."

"If he hit her because she caught him in the act, then it must have happened at a house," I said. "If she saw him in the woods by the lake there'd be no reason to kill her."

"Unless he's just a deranged murderer," she said. "She's alone in the woods, and he takes her out. Crime of opportunity."

"Why would a young girl go walking in the woods at night, over a mile from her cabin?"

"All the whys of this case are unanswered so far," she said. "That's where we come in."

Five

Officer Sally handed us a list of seventy addresses the next morning. He explained that he couldn't be sure they were all currently unoccupied. People come and go, and he didn't know everyone that owned a home on the mountain. He hadn't had enough time to research who owned each individual property.

"If we find something you'll probably need to contact the owners to give us more access," I said. "Until then, don't worry about it."

"It's a good list," he said. "All part-timers who haven't reported a previous break-in. All within the search area. Good luck."

"Thanks for your effort," I said. "I hope it pays off, but don't get your hopes up."

"We all feel bad that we can't do more to find the killer," he said. "And a little bit embarrassed that you two are doing our jobs for us."

"We've got the time," I said. "Brody's got the experience. It can't hurt if we poke around. Maybe we'll find something; maybe we won't."
"Better than us doing nothing," he said.

We sat drinking coffee and eating pastries while we compared the list to the map. Brody asked the Chief if we could make marks on the map of the properties to be searched.
"Take the map with you," he said. "Mark it up all you want. Just bring it back, so I have something to show for our efforts."
"Thanks, Chief," Brody said. "We'll take good care of it."

We went out to the car and used a marker to color the addresses we needed to visit. The Chief seemed more concerned with putting on a show for whoever might inquire than actually solving the crime. We didn't give a shit about that. I'd be happy to hand over the perp to him if it ever got that far. He could have all the credit he wanted. Brody and I were better off remaining anonymous.

Not being intimate with the neighborhood, we decided to drive around our route to get a feel for it and try to maintain a sense of direction. The first thing we did was get lost. We somehow managed to drive in a circle and end up where we'd started. It was not an encouraging start. The twisting mountain roads were confusing as hell. The side roads were all dead-ends. It was not a place to casually drive through with no particular destination. Eventually, we picked an address and found it. There were no cars in the driveway. We got out and started combing the property, concentrating on walkways and doors first.

It was clear that no one had been there recently, but that didn't rule it out. Our hermit would pick houses that he knew were unoccupied. Dead leaves covered the walkways. Nothing looked disturbed. Brody concentrated on the doors and sidewalks while I circled the property looking for anything that didn't belong. We found no clues.

We continued to search property after property all day long, coming up with nothing. We stopped off at the Chief's office on the way home to give him the addresses he could cross off his list. At the base of the mountain, we couldn't drive by Bodegas without stopping in for a beer. The waitress talked us into lobster rolls for dinner. Her recommendation was a good one.

"So this is good old fashioned police work," I said. "Pretty boring if you ask me."

"It is most of the time," she said. "It takes perseverance and patience. You sift through all the worthless fodder to find the one good piece of evidence. Took me many months to find you."

"I don't know that I want to spend months on this case," I said. "If we don't get a break in a few weeks I'm going to bag it."

"Never say never," she said. "We may get a small lead that takes us down another road. We keep following whatever the evidence gods give us until we hit a dead-end or solve the case."

"I'd feel more useful out in the wilderness doing the things that I'm good at," I told her. "Even if I came up empty."

"Without a crime scene there may as well be no crime," she said. "She wasn't killed out in the boonies unless it was down by the lake. I don't see her going there at night on her own. She's not from here. She probably didn't even know there was a lake on the mountain."

"Someone could have taken her there," I said. "Picked her up at the resort and went to do some drinking or necking or whatever."

"They would have done that in a car," she said. "That girl didn't voluntarily go off into the woods at night with a perfect stranger."

"We never considered the parking lot," I pointed out. "It was overrun with cars and people when we got there. It could have been the crime scene."

"Shit, you're right," she said. "I can't believe the cops didn't think of that right away."

"The Beech boys aren't investigators," I said. "Johnson isn't really a detective either. They did the best they could with what they had."

"We've still got an hour of daylight," she said. "Let's go back up there and scour the parking area and the park itself."

The park had seen heavy traffic since the girl's death. There was nothing to find in the gravel parking area but an abundance of tire tracks. The soft earth leading down to the water's edge had been trampled by hundreds of gawkers. The new spring grass had been flattened. Even the muddy spots had been walked through. I tried to visualize what might have happened. Some guy picks up the girl and drives her to this scenic spot. He plies her with alcohol or weed or romance. They walk down to the lake, and he smashes the back of her skull and kicks her in the water. It matched the timeline attached to the events of the next day. She drifted with the current towards the flow gates until the water level got too low and she grounded in the middle of the lake.

Finding evidence to match that scenario was a different story. Too many people had been here since then. The pool of potential evidence had been tainted. Brody was undeterred. She crawled on all fours along the shoreline, looking for blood or hair or anything that might be useful. I admired her determination, but the loss of light ended her search.

"Damn it," she said. "I was starting to get attached to the idea that she was killed right here. It makes the most sense."

"You want to come back tomorrow?" I asked. "Before we start going house to house again?"

"Yes, I do," she said. "Let's get an early start. If we're right, there could still be blood somewhere. That's about all that we could find that would be useful."

"Come on," I said. "Red is waiting for us."

It had been a long and fruitless day. Brody had done this before, but I hadn't. Just like Red, I liked to see some results for my efforts. I knew that I'd get tired of searching around those houses and finding nothing real fast. I suggested that we split up.

"Why don't I go back to looking for our hermit while you canvas the property list?" I asked.

"It will take me twice as long to do it by myself," she said.

"But our eggs are all in one basket," I countered. "We have two working theories."

"I think the guy picking her up at the resort scenario is the most likely," she said.

"I just have a gut feeling that the hermit is somehow connected," I said. "Finding traces of him while looking for her killer is too coincidental."

"Because you don't believe in coincidences," she said. "I see where you're coming from, but I have no such gut feeling."

"I'll go along for now," I said. "But I'm not giving up on the hermit. If we come up empty going through our list, I'll go after him."

"I know that's what you're good at," she said. "But you're as good as me looking for clues. You have the necessary awareness to make a good investigator. Most of us have to be taught that."

"It came with my lifestyle," I said. "Before I met you, situational awareness kept me alive."

"I've seen it first-hand since then," she said. "I've admired it, actually. You'll come in handy searching these properties. If there's anything to be found, we'll find it."

I wished there was a need for Red on Beech Mountain, but the park was full of conflicting scents that would only confuse him. I had to leave him at home while Brody and I returned to the park at first light. She focused her efforts on the shoreline, while I examined the perimeter of the grassy area. We gave it a solid three hours before giving up. There was no telltale blood splatter to be found.

We went back to work on the list, sometimes traveling by foot from house to house. All the properties started to look the same. The main feature was mountainous terrain with partially cleared woods. Most of the lots were less than half an acre, with minimal flat ground. There was a sidewalk or wooden walkway leading to the main entrance. Most provided decent privacy, even if the neighbors were close. In the dark, no one would see a damn thing from next door.

We crossed another ten houses off our list that day. I let Red out to run after we got home. He'd been missing his daily exercise sessions, so I let him wander the yard as long as he wanted. He finally decided that he was hungry, so we both joined Brody inside the cabin. I got a good fire going while Brody fixed dinner. It all seemed so normal. Looking in from the outside you'd never know we were working on a murder mystery during the day. We were simply enjoying a peaceful domestic life by night.

We weren't in Florida anymore. The drama of our life there overcame us. We had to escape or we'd lose our minds. I'd left a trail of trouble down there. Bad guys who'd prefer to see me dead, rescued maidens, one dead woman, high dollar drug deals, bullets flying; all of that was behind me now. In spite of the early difficulties I'd encountered in the mountains, we were finally settling into our new home. This mission could be left on Beech Mountain at the end of each day. No one was coming to our home to put us in danger.

That night I dreamt of the Beech Mountain Hermit, except he looked like my friend Pop. The old guy was frail and dirty, but he could move about the woods silently and unseen. I'd catch a glimpse of him, but then he'd disappear. No matter how hard I tried to track him, I failed. I knew he was there. I searched and searched, but never did find him.

The dream stuck with me after I woke. What made me think I could find the hermit? Sure, I'd gained some knowledge of the mountains and seemed to possess a certain aptitude for the woods, but this guy had survived in the wild for years without getting caught. He'd be infinitely better at the game I hoped to play with him. He'd probably laugh at the thought of me trying to catch him. The thought of it made me feel better about staying with Brody and working on our list.

Another day going house to house produced nothing but tired feet. We started having doubts about this line of attack. It seemed like a reasonable idea when we drew it up, but the real world results were disheartening.

"We just have to keep at it," she said. "Diligence creates opportunity."

"I think you've been to one too many inspirational speaker conferences," I said. "This is starting to look hopeless."

"If you lose hope you lose the case," she said. "I once spent a month staking out a suspect before I got what I needed."

"Our government pays people to sit in the bushes for a month?" I asked.

"Depends on the value of the target," she said. "The FBI is not involved in low-level crime."

"I wish we could set up a decoy house," I said. "We could sit inside comfortably and wait for the perp to come to us."

"Except he may never show," she said. "The break-ins have been infrequent. He's spread them out to keep the attention level low. I'd bet most of them were during severe weather. We should check on that."

"It's springtime now, or close enough," I said. "If the girl caught him red-handed, what was he doing here?"

"Who knows?" she said. "Maybe he just wanted to get a shower. Maybe he needed a new pair of socks. You don't have much confidence in that theory, do you?"

"If our hermit was involved, he wouldn't do it here," I said. "That's doesn't mean someone else didn't do it here. We're right to keep looking, but I'm not sold on any of our possible scenarios. Not enough evidence to support them."

"Not yet," she said. "That's what we're looking for."

"We missed the chance to get something at the park," I said. "I still think that's where it went down."

"It's hopelessly contaminated now," she said.

After five days we'd covered just over fifty properties. We kept crossing them off the list and moving on to the next one. We'd begun to learn our way around the neighborhood. We'd talked with a few curious neighbors, none of whom reported seeing the hermit or anything else unusual. Two of them were suspicious of our activities. A quick call to the police chief cleared that up for them.

Since the news of the girl's death had spread through the community, the police department took a dozen new calls reporting past break-ins or suspicious activity on their property. None of these events were recent. The homeowners had shown up for a weekend and noticed something odd. Originally, they didn't deem it necessary to report, but now they suddenly remembered it.

Mostly it was added fodder to a long list of non-leads.

Six

I let Red up on the couch so he could rest his head in my lap. I sat there stroking his fur and thinking. I stared at the fire, feeling a warm dog at my side. A pretty woman sat on the other side of Red, trying to learn how to hook a rug. I had a book, but I wasn't into it. The Beech Mountain mystery was foremost in my mind. I kept coming back to the hermit. Brody was right. I didn't believe in coincidences. He had to be connected somehow, even if it was only as a witness.

Maybe that was it. My gut told me to pursue the man, but that didn't necessarily mean he was the killer. We knew he came close to the park and the lake. We'd found a few of his haunts. I tried to piece a new scenario together in my head. The hermit came down to the lake after dark to bathe or pick through the trash cans or whatever. A car pulls in, and the girl and her killer get out. He watches what happens next. He's a witness to the crime but doesn't want to be discovered. He backtracks his trail to cover any trace, then disappears. The last thing he wants is for cops to start asking him questions.

Maybe he realized that he'd automatically become a suspect. His word wouldn't amount to much. He'd be an easy patsy for the police to lay the blame on. He didn't know the girl or feel any responsibility to help solve her murder. His main goal in life was to avoid society. Her death wouldn't change that. It might even intensify it. I was in the unique position to sympathize with him. Not only had I avoided society for a long time, but I'd also been friends with another hermit in these very mountains.

The difference between them and me was that I would have seen it as my responsibility to report what I'd witnessed. Hell, I'd taken responsibility for finding the killer even when I hadn't seen a thing. I still believed in justice, even if it was vigilante style. I knew right from wrong. I'd put myself in danger more than once to assure that justice was dealt out proportionately.

I made up my mind to find the hermit. I'd let the list play itself out. I'd stick with Brody on our search. Maybe we'd find some clue, some small piece of evidence that would direct us. Either way, I knew then that the hermit had to be found. I also knew that no one but me could find him.

On the sixth day, we almost had something. One of the properties had been disturbed, ever so slightly. We did not find a bloody rock or a broken window, but the subtle signs told us that someone had been there. The dusty door, surrounded by cobwebs, had a doorknob devoid of both of those things. There was also a handprint on the door frame, but no fingerprints. Someone wearing gloves had either entered or attempted entry. There were foot-shaped impressions in the mossy brick sidewalk. We got the Chief to call the owners, who reported that they hadn't been to their cabin in months.

With permission, the Beech Mountain PD entered the home to look around. Brody and I accompanied them. The Beech boys were one step above rent-a-cops, but Brody knew what to look for. She found an empty beer can in the otherwise empty trash can. The abundant dust was disturbed on the refrigerator door handle. The toilet seat was left up. There was still some water on the shower floor. Was it the hermit, or someone else? Who else could it be? Was it connected to the girl's murder in any way?

We couldn't answer those questions. The discovery only led to more unknowns. The entry didn't appear forced. Had the owners left the place unlocked? Was it someone who had a key? Did a family member or friend drop by unannounced to take a shower and steal a beer? We needed to question the owners, but we weren't actual investigators. We also didn't trust the Beech Mountain PD to ask the right questions in the manner that would elicit truthful responses.

"We need to know the identity of everyone who might have a key to this place," Brody announced. "Who owns this place, anyway?"

"The Chief knows them," an officer said. "Friends with them, I think."

"That's an interesting development," I said. "We'll need to talk with him, and them."

"I want to look around some more," Brody said. "There might be more here. Can I have some time alone in here?"

The officer had to ask the Chief, who permitted Brody to keep looking around. He left us alone with instructions to lock up when we were done. All of this was completely against any reasonable procedure. Why wasn't the Chief here himself? Why didn't we have some competent investigator on the scene? It was the location of a murder after all. The lack of vigor from local law enforcement was astounding, although I'd experienced it in the past. Murders were hard to solve, and beyond the capabilities of small-town departments here in northwest North Carolina. Resources were almost nonexistent, including forensic capabilities, manpower, and know-how.

I wondered how this would affect whatever else Brody might find. It seemed to me that a good defense lawyer would object to the chain of command of any evidence she uncovered. She forged ahead anyway, determined to find something more. I looked over the place too, but stayed out of her way. She was on a mission.

"The beds are undisturbed," she said. "He wasn't here long enough to take a dump, though he did take a leak. He drank a beer and took a shower. That's about it."

"No forcible entry," I said. "Came right in through the front door. This was not the hermit."

"It's someone known to this family," she said. "But that doesn't mean it's our killer."

"Another coincidence," I pointed out.

"Can't be sure how long ago he was here," she said. "With no one in the house, the shower could stay wet for a long time. The beer left in the can was stale and smelly. The toilet water wasn't particularly fresh. This could match up with our timeline. What if the killer came here to clean up afterward?"

"And he's someone the Chief knows," I said. "Shit's getting deeper."

"Yet the Chief granted us permission to keep sniffing around," she said. "That doesn't seem right."

"Should we turn over the scene to him?" I asked. "Or maybe call in the State Police?"

"Lacking a cellphone," she said. "We'll have to leave here to do either."

"Don't touch anything," I said. "We'll point out what you find to whoever comes in behind us."

"I wish I had some gloves," she said. "I'll be careful."

"The beer can will provide us with DNA," I said. "That officer should have bagged it."

"We're not dealing with a team of Sherlocks here," she said.

"One of the downsides to living in a crime-free zone," I said. "Top-notch investigators aren't needed around here. Not often anyway."

"Maybe I should open a private detective service," she said. "Contract out to the local departments. Put *Former FBI* on my business cards."

"I'll get some too," I said. "*Mountain man with a hound dog.*"

"Dynamic Duo Investigative Services," she said. "It's got a nice ring to it."

"Superheroes of the High Country," I added. "Able to leap small creeks with a single bound."

"Let me think for a minute," she said. "Guy waltzes in here with a key. Grabs a beer, takes a leak and a shower. We know it's a man because he left the toilet seat up. Doesn't appear to have disturbed anything else, unless he made the bed up real nice before he left. We need to check the fridge, the TV remote, and the toilet seat for prints. We need real cops for that, and a database."

"Keeping in mind that the Chief knows the homeowners here," I said. "Maybe even knows the person who entered. The casual nature of it suggests he was allowed to be here, and we've got no connection to the dead girl."

"But who drops by just to take a shower and then leaves?"

"Good point," I said. "Maybe a skier?"

"Certainly possible," she said. "We need to go find out what the Chief knows."

On the way to the police department, my gut started speaking to me again. It was telling me to be suspicious of the Chief. I tried to dismiss it, due to my previous trouble with the Banner Elk Chief. Not all cops were crooked, but the thought that we couldn't trust this guy wouldn't go away. Instead, it got louder and louder. Just before we pulled in the parking lot, I decided to drive on past.

"Where are we going?" Brody asked.

"Something's not right," I said. "I'm afraid the Chief will cover up whatever is found."

"Why?" she asked. "On what grounds?"

"Nothing but intuition," I confessed. "A gut feeling."

"But we need the police to take prints and run DNA," she said.

"I say we call Rominger or Johnson," I said. "I trust the state cops. We've got to get them involved."

"You want to let me in on the secret?"

"Just a bullshit theory," I said. "For the purpose of argument, let's say this mystery person is our killer. After he offed the girl, he went to that address to clean up. The owners are friends with the Chief. The suspect may be known to the Chief. He goes in and dismisses or falsifies the evidence to protect someone unknown to us. We'll never know the truth."

"First rate conspiracy theory," she said. "Based on nothing."

"I listen to my gut," I told her. "It has served me well."

"That's everything the FBI taught us not to do," she said. "Never let your personal feelings interfere with the evidence."

"So far our evidence is incomplete," I said. "We know someone was in that house, but we don't know who. If we leave it up to the Chief, we may never know."

"Just like we don't know the identity of the Beech Mountain Hermit," she said. "We're no closer to solving this murder than when we started."

"Chasing coincidences," I said. "I hate it, but it's all we've got."

"While the cops all sit drinking coffee and eating donuts," she said. "It's a wonderful place we've moved to."

"Gives us something to do," I said. "Sure beats cleaning poop out of the bilge."

"Or getting eaten alive by mosquitoes," she said. "Or any number of other things we used to deal with."

"The only thing constant in life is change," I said. "We've made a big one. Any regrets?"

"Not a damn one," she said. "I love our cabin. It's beautiful here. The cold didn't defeat us. I'm content with the move."

"Me too," I said. "Now let's go find some real cops."

We drove from Beech Mountain to Boone to visit the State Police. Johnson was off duty, but Rominger was out on the roads. He came back in to hear our concerns. I told him what we'd found and presented him with our various theories.

"We think it would be best if you guys took control up there," I said. "Collect the evidence properly and maintain the chain of custody so it can be used later if it proves useful."

"You say your gut tells you not to trust the Chief of Police on Beech Mountain," he said. "But does it tell you that this person was indeed the killer?"

"It doesn't say either way," I said. "But I'm inclined to follow this lead until we've got some proof. We clear the guy and move on, or he's our killer."

"What about the hermit?" he asked. "You were all fired up about him at first."

"I didn't know he existed before I started digging around in the woods," I said. "Hell, we're all assuming that what I found is connected to the break-ins. There's a whole lot of assuming going on. We have evidence that a man sometimes sleeps in the woods near the lake. We have no evidence that he breaks into houses, or that he killed the girl. We have evidence that someone entered this particular house and took a shower. We have nothing to connect him to the murder either. It's my personal opinion that the Chief on Beech Mountain does not have the skill nor the resources to solve this particular crime, and may even have the incentive to cover it up."

"That's where we come in?" he asked.

"My opinion is more professional than personal," Brody said. "But I know Breeze well enough to give credence to his hunches."

"You two have learned more about what's going on up there than the rest of us," he said. "I'll give you that much. But it's still damn little to go on."

"Figure out who was in that house and what he was doing there," Brody said. "Maybe his visit is perfectly innocent. Won't hurt our feelings. We'll look elsewhere, but with so little to go on, we can't let this particular clue slip out of our hands."

"I agree," he said. "Let me make my commander aware. We'll move in on the Chief's turf and take over."

"We've got a few more properties on the list," I said. "Then I think I might try to locate our hermit."

"That's on you," he said. "Did you get a phone yet?"

"Don't intend to," I told him.

"Makes it difficult to communicate with you," he said. "Fucking dinosaur."

"I am what I am," I said. "We can dig out the SAT phone if you want."

"Would you?" he asked. "I'm going to need to contact you sooner or later."

"Okay, fine," I said. "We'll go home and charge the thing up. We'll be up on Beech tomorrow. After that, I'll be out west of the lake. Let us know who was in that house."

"Will do."

We drove home with nothing but questions that had no answers. We had no murder weapon, no crime scene, and no real suspects. We'd been trying to connect random events to the girl's murder. There was official police work to be done at the house someone had entered, but it could have been a legitimate visitor having nothing to do with the crime. There was an unknown individual frequenting the woods around the lake. He may or may not be the person responsible for multiple break-ins over a course of years.

Our good old-fashioned shoe leather approach wasn't producing much in the way of results. The Beech Mountain officers who'd interviewed various random people at the ski resort hadn't discovered much either. Yes, the girl had been spotted by several guests, but no one saw her leave, with or without a man. She'd barely been on anyone's radar before she vanished.

No one had come forward to offer any eyewitness information. No one saw her at the lake. No one saw her along the streets of the town. We couldn't place her anywhere but at the ski village. Most of the guests from that night were now long gone. This was no Agatha Christie mystery where all the guests were locked in the lodge until the crime was solved. People came from all over the world to ski on Beech Mountain. The local cops hadn't spoken with all of them. Once they found the kids who remembered the girl, they hadn't dug much deeper.

If you want your murder to be solved, don't get killed in northwestern North Carolina. The small local agencies and the county Sheriffs aren't equipped to successfully investigate murders unless the culprit is obvious. In the case of the girl's death, nothing was obvious. It appeared to be a random murder with no motive. The girl had no connection to anyone local. Anyone she met at the resort would have been a stranger. That didn't make her any less dead, but it made finding her killer practically impossible.

Brody held out hope that either we'd find something at one of the last few houses on our list, or what we'd already found would lead to the killer. I had little confidence in either. I wasn't contributing much to the search; it wasn't my area of expertise. I felt like I was on a leash. My place was out in the wilderness tracking down the hermit. He might not have killed the girl, but his existence was part of this mystery. I didn't care about his habit of entering vacant houses for a little comfort. I wasn't trying to have him prosecuted for that. I wanted to meet the man and take a measure of him.

He was of the mountains like I aspired to be. He knew the wild ways of the High Country. He was a survivor. Maybe he killed the girl, maybe he didn't, but I couldn't know until I found him. I did know that he'd been near the lake sometime around the time of her death. Red wouldn't have picked up his scent otherwise. Maybe he saw something that would be helpful to the case. Maybe he could identify the person who dumped the girl's body. Either way, I was now determined to find the Beech Mountain Hermit. It was the best way I could think of to contribute to the effort.

First I had to endure another day of walking the properties on the list. Brody was just as diligent as she'd been on the first day. I tried to concentrate, but my mind was elsewhere. We didn't find one damn thing out of the ordinary that day, and I was done with it.

"Let's get in touch with Rominger," I said. "See what's happening on his end."

Seven

We didn't like what Rominger had to say. The Chief had been uncooperative. It was his jurisdiction, and he'd be damned if the State Police would interfere in his investigation. He was friends with the homeowners, and it was his duty to find out what was going on at their property. No one had a key. No one had permission to enter in their absence. They didn't hide a key on the premises.

He failed to mention that he'd ceded the early investigation to civilians, or that he'd shown no interest in the crime whatsoever until this particular address became an issue. He did admit that he hadn't yet found the time to go collect any evidence from the scene.
"We need to get in there and get that beer can," I said. "And dust for prints. The Chief will cover it up."
"But why?" Brody asked. "And what good is the evidence if we take it with no police presence?"

"Help me out here, Rominger," I said. "Can't you get a warrant or something?"

"That address is solidly within the town limits of Beech Mountain," he said. "They've got jurisdiction over the lake and right up to the Watauga River to the north."

"In Watauga County?" I asked.

"Most of it is in Avery County," he said. "But parts are in Watauga."

"So how do we get the beer can and take prints and still be able to use them?"

"I don't see a way," he said. "But maybe your concerns about the Chief are overblown. Maybe he is just protecting his turf here. He didn't much care until you found something, but now he's on the case."

"Goes against my gut," I told him. "That's all I can tell you."

"I can't force him to turn over the evidence to us," he said. "He's got first right."

"Can you follow up on it?" I asked. "Have him tell you who the person was?"

"If he makes a clear determination," he said. "We're obviously an interested agency on this case."

"I already don't trust him," I said. "Why do I think he'll say he found no matches to DNA or fingerprints?"

"At that point, we'll ask to run the search ourselves," he said. "He'll have to share it with us."

"Bingo," I said. "So we wait for him to bungle it, then you can look into it further."

"If he cooperates," he said. "Which is what he didn't do today."

"You know where I stand," I said. "But I'm done dicking around here. I'm going after the hermit. Let us know what the Chief gives you."

"That ought to keep you out of our hair for a while," he said. "Let us do our job, Breeze. We can't take your gut to court."

The wheels of justice were turning way too slowly for my taste, but there was nothing I could do about it. Finding the hermit wouldn't necessarily speed things up either. I also knew that locating one anonymous man in a vast wilderness was like playing the lottery. The odds were not in my favor.

As far as I was concerned, the only good thing about Beech Mountain was the brewery in the ski village. Too many houses had been built over the years. The roads were treacherous. I didn't like to ski, but mainly I was pissed that no one seemed serious about solving the murder of a teenage girl from France. At least I had Brody on my side.

"Is it always like this?" I asked her. "Competing agencies?"

"If the FBI moved in on a case, it was theirs," she said. "No matter how much the locals protested. This is different."

"Clearly the State Police are better equipped," I said.

"But the agency having jurisdiction has to request their aid," she said. "That happens all the time with small towns. Some of them can't even provide service twenty-four seven, especially in rural areas, who generally would call in the Sheriff's Department."

I wondered which county our suspect property was in. Involving Avery County would reintroduce Angelina Will to the case. I'd had mixed results with the Watauga County Sheriff's Department. Their former Sheriff had hated me. He'd lost his reelection bid. Since then I'd been called by them to help with a case. Red had solved it in short order, but I wasn't close to anyone there. The deputy I'd assisted would vouch for me, but I couldn't even remember his name.

The devil on my left shoulder told me to call Avery County. He knew I wanted to see Angelina again. The angel on my right shoulder had a different opinion. He knew that I didn't need the type of temptation that she would bring. Both of them were right.

I'd have to let things play out with the Beech Mountain Chief of Police and hope that he had integrity, or that Rominger could somehow get involved. They were the law, and I was not. At least Rominger had told the Chief what to look for. It would be hard for him to make the beer can disappear at this point. He could replace it with another one though, if he were that devious. I was letting my past interactions with a crooked cop influence my opinion of the man. I needed to step away from the whole thing and let the real authorities do their job.

Brody was finally starting to share my frustration. She'd been certain that we'd find more clues by working that list of properties. It was a well-thought-out plan, I gave her that, but our part of its execution was now over. "I hate coming up short," she said. "If I had a police force under my control we would have solved this case by now."

"Maybe the unannounced intruder will turn out to be our guy," I suggested. "In that case, we were integral in solving the crime."

"I'm starting to smell something funny about the situation up there too," she said. "It's not the same as your gut feeling, but the fact that the Chief knows the homeowners is highly suspicious."

"We'll know more soon," I said. "Rominger will stay on him about it."

"You still planning on chasing a ghost through the wilderness?" she asked.

"You're welcome to tag along," I said. "Work on your backwoods skills."

"I'm almost inclined to accept your invitation," she said.

"Almost?"

"But I know what will happen," she continued. "After a while, you'll be dressed like Jed Clampett and sleeping under a log. I'm going to have to pass."

"For starters, I'm just going to do some hiking," I said. "Maybe take Red along on a few trips. Get to know the land, find my way around."

"I can deal with that," she said. "But as soon as you get too serious with your Zen stuff, I'll stay home."

"Deal," I said. "We'll take tomorrow off to do something fun. Start the next day."

"You want to drive down to Looking Glass Falls, or maybe Dry Falls?" she asked. "Make a day of it?"

"Sure, sounds good," I said. "Give our minds a break. Enjoy life."

Looking Glass Falls was near Brevard, in the Pisgah National Forest. It took us over two hours to get there, but it was worth it. It was easy to access and arguably the most beautiful waterfall we'd seen. We still had plenty of time left in the day, so we drove on to Dry Falls, near Highland. It was just off the side of Highway 64 and a short walk. The water runs off a high cliff, allowing you to walk behind it without getting wet. We could feel the power of the rushing water as we stood behind it. It would have been even more fantastic if we didn't have to share with fifty or so other folks. Still, both falls were well worth the drive.

We enjoyed the scenery on the way home, talking about anything other than the dead girl on Beech Mountain. We discussed ways we might improve life at our little creekside cabin. Brody wanted a garden, but we lacked flat land that wasn't pure rock underneath. I wanted a woodshed. We could keep our firewood dry without lugging it up to the porch. A snow blower would be nice to have, but it wasn't deemed a necessity. We'd only been snowed in a few times, and we weathered those events just fine.

We decided to stop for dinner at Stonewalls in Banner Elk. During the height of the ski season, you couldn't get in the place without a reservation, but traffic had slowed and we were able to get a table. The special was Chilean Sea Bass, which was excellent. Brody got the shrimp scampi. I paid eight bucks for a craft beer, which irritated me to no end. I could drink six beers at home for that and have a few bucks left over. It was a nice experience though. The ban on talk of the dead girl stayed in effect.

It was late when we got home, but I built a fire anyway. I took Red out to do his thing. When I came back in, I found Brody in sexy negligee lying on a blanket in front of the fireplace. Red got locked in a bedroom. The next twenty minutes were spent trying to add some steam to the heat of the fire.

The heat from the fireplace kept the light sweat we both had on our skin from causing a chill. It created an odd sensation of cooling off while keeping warm that I can't say I'd experienced before. It stimulated us to go for round two, something we hadn't accomplished in quite some time. It was satisfying enough to eliminate the need to try for round three.

We put on robes and stowed the blanket away before letting Red out of jail. He was happy that we were both home. We gave him some good doggy loving before turning in for the night. It had been a long and enjoyable day, the kind of day we'd moved to the mountains to experience. I don't know about Brody, but I got the best night of sleep I'd had in forever. I had dreams, but they were all pleasant.

Nightmares had haunted me in the past. They all involved death. First, it was the death of my wife, Laura. Later it was a dead woman in my arms on the streets of Miami. Then it was the man I'd beaten to death down in Guatemala. They came back to torment me in my sleep. Since the move to the Blue Ridge Mountains, they'd stopped, for which I was grateful. To me, it meant that I'd successfully run away from my past.

One of the dreams that night involved the Beech Mountain Hermit. Again, he looked like my dead friend Pop. We sat and talked by a clear mountain stream like we were old friends. I sensed no danger in his presence. At first glance, he looked old and feeble, but when he moved it was quick and lithe. It was also silent. He was so light on his feet that he could have been weightless.

That part of the dream stuck with me after I woke. I wanted to go track the man down, but how? Could he really move like that? If he was that good, how could I expect to find him? The depth of my sleep made me a bit sluggish. It took an extra cup of coffee to shake it off. I told Brody about how well I'd slept, and about the hermit dream.

"You're super curious about this guy, aren't you?" she asked.

"I am," I said. "I admit it. I admire people like him. I don't want to live like that, but yes, I'm curious."

"Good, because if you want to sleep in caves, you'll be doing it by yourself."

"You're the reason I don't want to live like that," I said. "I not only want to be with you, but I also want you to be comfortable and happy."

"I am both," she said. "Let's keep it that way."

After a leisurely breakfast, we got a late start up Beech Mountain. I wanted Brody to participate, so I didn't push her. We started at the park by the lake and made a quick swing through the area I'd already searched with Angelina. I showed her the spots we figured the hermit had been. From there we followed the trail Red had been on before losing it at the water's edge.

"It's almost like you were close to him, actually on his heels," she said. "He went into the lake to shake you off."

"Except there was no water in the lake at the time," I said. "We'd have seen footprints in the mud."

"Then he went so far as to lose a tail that he didn't even have," she said. "Like he knew someone would come after him soon."

"He couldn't know I'd come with a hound dog," I said.

"He's been surviving here for years without being seen," she said. "He's got to be extremely cautious."

"That is pretty extreme," I agreed. "He's moving through the area but takes steps to hide his trail even though no one is after him. That's a whole new level of precaution."

"You are a tracker," she said. "One with special skills. You found his little stopover points, but it's not likely anyone else would have."

"He covered them well," I said. "I got lucky."

"You make your own luck," she said. "We know that. You found clues of his existence once; you can do it again."

"There are thousands of acres to hide beyond here," I said.

"This is what you've been wanting," she replied. "What do we do next?"

"I think we need to cover some ground," I said. "Stay aware but not focusing on the little things. He's not holed up near here. He's got to have a safe place away from civilization."

"Let's get hiking," she said. "Before we come back we need to figure out more access points. We'll end up many miles from the lake eventually."

"We still have that map," I said. "We can figure out the roads. We'll just need to find a place to park."

We got to the place where Red had lost the trail. Trees grew right to the edge of the lake. The undergrowth was too thick to push through. I wasn't up to wading in the water, but I guessed that the hermit simply went around this section of thicket to a more navigable part of the woods. We backtracked and looked for a dry way around the obstacle. We ended up going far out of our way to get back down to the water again, but we found the going much easier. I stopped to study the bank and soft earth beside the lake. I almost didn't notice it, but there it was; a footprint.

The reason I nearly missed it was because there was no tread imprint. It was a flat, featureless shape of a shoe, just barely indenting the ground.

"What kind of shoe has zero tread?" I asked Brody.

"Dress shoes for one," she said. "But I'd say we can rule that one out. Moccasins maybe?"

"Those slipper things that Indians wore?"

"They still make them," she said. "They're all the rage with the hipster crowd."

"The Hipster Hermit of Beech Mountain," I said. "I don't think it will sell."

"Maybe he has Indian blood," she said. "That's where his skills come from."

"Or maybe he saw a nice pair in someone's vacant cabin and couldn't resist."

"Either way, it's our first clue," she said. "He came this way."

"At least we think he did," I said. "A casual hiker wouldn't use the lake to go around an obstacle like this. It's a good tactic though. Plus it shows how well he knows these woods."

"Just a few hundred thousand more acres to search," she said. "Piece of cake."

"Let's think about this," I said. "He wouldn't want to walk twenty miles to get to town. He'd want to be somewhere far from the nearest house, but close enough to keep his commute manageable."

"How did Pop get food and the occasional necessity?" she asked.

"He was less than five miles from Banner Elk," I said. "But in a place with no houses nearby. Cody Banner's place was the closest, but it was a hunting camp, not a full-time residence."

"Richard and us were his closest neighbors then," she said.

"No doubt about it," I said. "But we were several miles away."

"We're several miles from downtown right where we are," she pointed out.

"True enough," I said. "But not from the nearest house. Plus the park has a lot of traffic. You've got the lake and the community center right there. He has to come through here to get to those cabins, but he's not living here."

"Then how do we know which way to go next?"

"We don't," I admitted. "Let's slow this down and start paying closer attention. See if we can't pick up another clue nearby."

"Split up?"

"Yes, but stay close enough to communicate," I said. "No point in one of us getting lost out here."

We fanned out and began searching the immediate area, looking for another print or some sign of habitation. If we could find a broken branch, discarded apple core, anything that would reveal the previous presence of a person, we could refocus our efforts. Two hours later Brody whistled. I went to her, and she pointed down at the ground.

"What?" I asked.

"I think that's a partial print," she replied.

"Where?"

She got down on one knee and stuck her finger in an impression in the ground. I could barely make it out, but it was half of the same imprint we'd seen earlier.

"How'd you ever find that?" I asked.

"It jumped out at me," she said. "Just lucky I guess."

"Damn good find," I told her. "You'll be a full-fledged woodsman yet."

"I think it's a woodsperson these days," she said. "Wouldn't want to be non-PC."

"You found another clue," I said. "He came this way. Look back towards where we found the first one and figure out which way he was going."

That was harder than it sounds. We were on mountainous terrain in thick woods. The lake was below us, but we'd taken a circuitous route to get here, wandering around looking for any hint of the hermit. I went back the way we'd come for a few hundred yards, leaving Brody standing at the new print. I used my arm like I was sighting down a rifle. I examined the woods behind her, trying to determine the most likely path.

"Almost straight up from where you are," I said. "See that line of rocks going up to the ridge?"

"I'll go up on the left," she said. "You take the right."

She started up before I got to her, so I continued up the hill on the right side of the rocks. They were a jumbled mess of jagged edges and slick moss-covered surfaces. As a hiker, I wouldn't try to use them to walk on. Either side of them would be a much easier travel lane.

"Don't go too fast," I said. "Keep your eyes down. Look for another footprint."

"Got it."

I followed my advice. If we found something, we'd have reason to stay on track. If we didn't, we wouldn't know if he came this way or not. We'd have to go back down and look around until we discovered some other trace of the man. If I'd been by myself, I'd have to go back down and try again on Brody's side of the rocks. I was glad to have her with me.

I was three-quarters of the way to the ridge when I thought I'd found something. It was so faint I could have imagined it. The soil was no deeper than an inch, but my eyes made out the toe portion of that moccasin print, with no heel. I climbed a few more steps, watching my feet and how they landed. Sure enough, only the forefoot and toe touched the ground. I went back to the semi-print and called Brody.

"I may have something," I said. "Can you climb over or do you need to go to the top?"

"Give me a few minutes," she said.

"Nice and easy," I said. "Don't take any chances."

She made it over the rock line with care and caution. I showed her what I'd found.

"That's less obvious than the last one," she said. "Good eye."

"So we know he came up this side," I said. "We keep putting the pieces together, step by step."

"Except it's getting late," she said. "We've still got to walk all the way back to the car."

"Let me get on top of the ridge and look around," I said. "Then we'll head back."

"Coming with," she said.

Eight

We climbed the last two hundred feet together and stood up on the ridge. It felt like we could see for a hundred miles. Out in front of us was a vast wilderness. An occasional cabin was set back in the woods or on top of a rise. The town of Elk Park, North Carolina, was to our south. Roan Mountain, Tennessee was to the southwest. Watauga Lake was to our north. Directly to our west was a whole lot of nothing. Our hermit was out there somewhere.

Finding him seemed an impossible undertaking, even more so than before. Thousands of acres of untouched wilderness spread out before us. There were few roads, and we weren't able to figure out where they came from. We'd need to drive through there to find new places to embark from if we could discern where they were. I took mental bearings on the small towns and the big lake. I felt that I could figure it out with a good map, but a handheld GPS would really be the ticket. Shouldn't be hard to find in an area where hiking was the number one pastime.

I was satisfied with what we'd learned and what we'd found so far. It had been a productive day, much more so than I had expected.
"So this is how you do it?" asked Brody. "Walk around looking for clues and bam; there's a footprint?"
"I use Zen mode when I know I'm closing in," I said. "I start hearing, seeing and smelling on a higher level."
"This guy is going to challenge that ability," she said. "Just getting close to him is going to be difficult."
"Let's not get ahead of ourselves," I said. "I'll worry about his skills when the time comes. We've got a lot of land to cover first."
"Do you think he could be here right now?" she asked. "Watching our every move?"
"I suppose it's possible," I said. "But I don't sense it. We're not close, yet."
"Your gut talking?"
"That and jumping to some logical conclusions," I said. "There's no cover up this high. He's down below us, probably in the middle zone between and away from populated areas."

She pointed down to the valley below us, moving her finger back and forth.

"If that theory holds, it certainly narrows the search area," she said. "Do you think Red could help?"

"He needs something to go on," I said. "A piece of clothing. He prefers socks."

"Or a fresh trail, right?" she asked. "If you come upon a recent track, he can follow it."

"Apparently," I said. "We had a fresh scent down close to the lake that day. The one that disappeared into the water, or mud."

"But we'll never know when we might stumble onto a fresh scent," she said. "We could find something and not have the dog with us."

"That's a lot of we and us," I said. "I thought you were going to bail on me when I got close."

"I'm split on the issue," she said.

"How so?"

"I'm getting personally invested in finding this guy now," she said. "But I don't want to distract you when you get all Zen. I'd become a liability when the real tracking begins."

"Even Red will be a liability if it gets down to me and the hermit in the woods," I said. "He'll know a dog is coming. Red will give me away from a mile off."

"But we're nowhere near that point yet," she said. "So I keep helping you zero in. Let me know when I need to retreat."

"Maybe I can have you stage out there somewhere," I suggested. "I might need some backup, or even rescue."

"We need two-way radios," she said. "We can probably get them at the same place we get a GPS."

"Better than smartphones," I said. "Good old walkie-talkies."

"Next I'll talk you into a TV," she said. "With cable."

"That's a discussion for another day," I said. "We should head back. We've done well."

We didn't waste time looking for additional clues on the hike back. We had some groundwork to take care of before we returned. After we picked up the additional equipment and drove through the area we wanted to search, we'd return. I wanted time to thoroughly study a good map too. I weighed the pros and cons of having our hound dog with us. I felt like we'd reduced the potential acreage to search significantly, which was a positive development. I also wondered what the Beech Mountain Chief was doing.

After we got home, I plugged the SAT phone into the charger, anticipating a call from Rominger. I was dying to know if there had been any progress on the mystery intruder on Beech Mountain. If that lead led to the killer, there would be no need to continue looking for the hermit. Don't get me wrong, half of me desperately wanted to find the man, but half of me was afraid of failure. I was still relatively new to these mountains. I'd discovered a skill I never knew that I possessed, a talent really, but we assumed that the hermit was a true expert. In fact, in my mind, I'd bestowed him with mythical skills. I wasn't sure I could beat him.

We drove down to Valle Crucis the next day to see what Mast General Store had to offer. They stocked several varieties of handheld GPS units designed for hikers. They also had two-way radios that were very small and light. We got what we needed in one stop, except for a good topographic map. We struggled with that. They were available online, but we didn't own a computer. Brody finally suggested that we try the library. We were able to print several different versions for a small fee.

We then drove through Banner Elk heading west towards Tennessee on NC 194. From the small town of Elk Park, we drove onto Walnut Mountain Road, which took us into the Cherokee Wildlife Management Area, which straddled the Tennessee and North Carolina border. This was the place to access the wilderness area we'd seen from the top of that ridge the day before. We continued to drive, taking note of places to pull off the road. There were a few state managed trailheads with small dirt parking lots that we could utilize. I marked each one on a map for future reference.

We weren't actually in the woods searching for a ghost, but we were laying a foundation for our hunt. I felt good about it. My gut told me that the hermit was in the Cherokee forest. It was just down the mountain from Buckeye Lake and the homes that had been broken into, but it was undeveloped. Hiking up that side of Beech was no picnic, but it wouldn't deter a longtime mountain man like our hermit.

We went home to our cabin to study the new maps and prepare for long mountain hikes. I spread everything out on the kitchen table, and it reminded me of how I used to study marine charts anytime I was about to take the boat to someplace new. I had a fine chart plotter on the boat, but I always relied on paper charts to plan my trips in advance. I had to take our new GPS outside for it to pick up satellites. It was not a sophisticated model, but it would keep us from getting lost, and we could mark waypoints if necessary.

Brody tested the two-way radios, before handing me one and telling me to start walking and talking. I made it more than a half-mile before we started losing contact. I was sure they'd work further apart if we had a clear line of sight with each other, but the mountain rocks limited the signal's reach.

I loaded backpacks with bottled water and high-energy snacks while Brody fixed dinner. After we ate, she gave our handguns a good cleaning, even though they were already spotless. She was serious about our gun maintenance, so I let her do her thing. She proved early on that she was a much better shot than I was with handguns. I learned from her and got better, but she'd still whip me in a competition. I took solace in the fact that I was way better with a rifle than her. I could hit a stationary target at incredible distances, sniper-like.

We were ready for an extended hunt for a man we'd never seen. As far as we knew, no one had ever seen the hermit. When I thought too hard on that fact, I found it humorous. Did he even exist? Were we about to embark on the most epic wild goose chase ever? I tried to ground myself with all the reports of break-ins on Beech Mountain and the few clues I'd found down by the lake.

Everything made sense, except for the complete lack of eyewitnesses.

We'd just spent good money on radios, a GPS and various maps, all to hunt someone who may not even be real. I couldn't help myself. I laughed out loud.

"What's so funny?" Brody asked.

"We're going on a Bigfoot hunt," I said. "Looking for the Loch Ness Monster."

"What are you talking about?"

"When I was a teenager, we told stories about the Hook Man of Blackbird Forest," I told her. "We'd heard those stories from previous generations. It was a myth, but it persisted. There are probably kids there now talking about Hook Man."

"You think the hermit is an imaginary creature?"

"Actually, I don't," I said. "But it struck my funny bone to think that he might be."

"You have a strange sense of humor," she said. "All this time I thought this was serious business."

"The girl's murder is certainly serious business," I said. "That's why we're trying to help."

"We're now focused on this questionable hermit," she said. "We've been excluded from the police work. What makes us think he had anything to do with it? Tell me why we're looking for him again."

"We know he was near the lake at the time of the killing," I said. "Or at the time she was dumped. Red was on his trail. His scent was fresh."

"That makes him a suspect," she said. "Opportunity for one, but the mystery of the man too."

"Which isn't logical," I said. "We have no basis to suspect him without evidence. We either find the evidence, or we find the man."

"And he could have been a witness," she said. "If he was there when the body was dumped."

"Which he would be in no hurry to report," I said. "He wouldn't want to expose himself."

"He's gone all these years without being seen," she said. "He can't come forward now."

"Exactly."

"So we find him," I said. "Then find out what he knows. Maybe we'll discover something tying him to the girl. Maybe he'll tell us what he saw."

"Or who he saw," she added.

I spent some quality time with my hound dog after dinner. I'd been neglecting him lately, but he was a very tolerant type. He was happy to share me with Brody and allowed me other pursuits besides playing the missing sock game. I hoped to be able to include him in the hermit search at some point. If I could manage to get something with the mystery mountain man's scent on it, Red would find him a lot quicker than I ever could.

We'd been too busy. I took some time to sit by the fire, Red's head in my lap, and read a good book. I was on book three in the Chase Fulton Series by Cap Daniels. It was full of boats and tropical locations that took me back to my Florida days. His hero was new at his work, much like I was. He overcame his inexperience and an occasional mistake with quick thinking and decisive action. Chase Fulton kept moving towards his goal, staying aware, overcoming obstacles, and following clues until his mission was complete. It was a satisfying read that kept me up a bit late.

I had an unsatisfying dream that night. It was an endless walk through the woods. Walking, walking, and walking for miles and miles. There was no hermit. There were no clues. There were trees and rocks and flora and fauna, but that was it. I walked what seemed like forever in my dream and found nothing at all. It felt like Forrest Gump running across the country for no reason at all. Just running and running with no end in sight.

Thankfully, I didn't feel tired from all the walking I'd done in my dream the next morning. I felt refreshed, but my doubts had been renewed.

"Tell me the truth," I said to Brody. "Is there any chance at all of finding this guy?"

"I think the odds are long," she said. "But if anyone can do it, it's you."

"How long?" I asked. "Am I wasting my time?"

"This is where I tell you that a walk in the woods is never a waste of time," she said. "Or some other inspirational platitude."

"Seriously," I said. "Can I do this?"

"I don't recall you ever doubting yourself," she said. "It's not in your make-up."

"Oh, I've doubted myself plenty," I said. "I just never let it show. Now I've got you to bounce my thoughts off of."

"Expand your thinking on this mission," she said. "What's bothering you?"

"You remember how you said you were split on the issue of going with me?" I asked. "I'm split on the idea of finding the hermit. It's a fantastic challenge that I jumped at. It would be definitive proof of my new-found skills. It would validate everything I've become since moving here."

"What's the downside?" she asked. "You don't find him. There's nothing lost, except maybe a blow to your ego.

If you do find him, you're a hero, solver of the great Beech Mountain Hermit Mystery. You'll be a legend."

"Won't matter much if it doesn't lead to the girl's killer," I said. "If it wasn't for her, I'd leave the hermit alone. Let him live his life the way he's chosen."

"You didn't leave Pop alone," she said.

"Pop found me when I stumbled into his pot farm," I said. "I'd have never been able to find him, at least not back then. I learned from him."

"Which again proves that you're the man for the job," she pointed out. "Who else is going to find a reclusive mountain man that can move like smoke?"

"You're right," I said. "Unless we hire another ghost man of the mountains, no one has any chance to catch this man. I'm as good as it gets. If I fail, I'll have to deal with it, but I've got to try."

"Go get 'em, champ," she said, slapping me on the ass.

Her encouragement was just what I needed that morning. She made me realize that I was enough of a man to manage the disappointment if I failed, but that I was uniquely equipped for this particular mission. She didn't offer me an out. She could have told me that I didn't need the aggravation. She could have reminded me that I was a volunteer, free to bow out whenever I chose. Instead, she convinced me that I needed to do this thing. That I could do this thing.

We got an early start, driving to one of the dirt parking lots inside the Cherokee Wildlife Management Area. I fired up the little GPS, and Brody turned on our radios. The walkie-talkies would allow us to spread out further if it became necessary. We put our packs on our backs and made tracks into the woods. We followed the obvious trail until we were deep into the woods. Using the GPS, we veered off the trail towards our intended search area. The farther we got from the established trail, the thicker the vegetation became. It slowed us down considerably. I remembered the machete that I'd seen at Mast General Store and regretted not buying it.

We trudged along without it, still feeling strong. All of our earlier hiking expeditions had prepared us well. Our mountain legs hadn't come easy, but I was thankful for them now. Brody didn't complain in the least. We kept putting one foot in front of the other, diving deeper and deeper into the wilderness. After a steep uphill climb, we stopped to rest.
"Where are we?" Brody asked.

"About a mile southwest of that ridge where we stopped last time," I said. "On the southern edges of our potential search area."
"Do we pick up where we left off?"
"Unless you have a better idea," I said.

That mile was an up and down affair, taxing our legs even further. We didn't have time to look closely for clues along the way. We wanted to make it to our last position and then start looking in earnest. Our man could have gone in many different directions from the top of the ridge, but I was positive that he'd gone down. His hideout would be in an area of heavy cover, far from the prying eyes of the stray hiker.

We rested again at the top of the ridge. It was a good long break that we both needed. We ate and drank and let our muscles recover.
"So we think he went down from here," Brody said. "Straight down, or in some other direction?"
"Easiest to go straight," I said. "But he's exhibited the will to throw off any trackers before. I'd have to guess that he took some other direction."
"Let me see the GPS," she said.

She studied it briefly before handing it back to me.

"Straight down is due west," she said. "Into the middle of the wildest zone. Seems like he'd go there."

"But he wouldn't necessarily choose a straight path," I said. "It's a crapshoot from here."

"I don't know," she said. "We're pretty far out here. Why would he think someone would follow him this far from civilization?"

"He didn't stay anonymous this long without being paranoid," I said. "Straight down is too obvious. He went north or south from this point. He can always circle back to center down there in the valley."

"What's your gut telling you?"

"North," I said. "There are two towns to the southwest. Nothing to the north but Watauga Lake."

"Why would he frequent Buckeye Lake if Watauga Lake was closer to home?" she asked.

"Not much there but the marina," I said. "Breaking into boats is a sure way to get caught. Anyone on the docks would know who belonged and who didn't."

"All those easy empty houses on Beech are a much more inviting target," she said.

"Just far enough away from his home base," I speculated. "The cops ain't coming out here."

"You want to split up?" she asked. "I'll let you take the northern route."

"Gee thanks," I said. "Once you get to the valley floor, move back towards the middle. We'll use the radios to meet up eventually. You ready for this?"

"Ready," she said.

Nine

I started my descent, angling to the north, while Brody did the opposite. Now we were actively searching for signs of the hermit's passage. We still had half the day to look around. We were entering the mystery man's turf. We were on his terms from here on out. I tried to put myself in his shoes. The base of the ridge, down there on flat ground, seemed a likely place to hide from people. He'd need shelter of some kind, far from established trails, but close enough to those vulnerable cabins. There would be no point in having a base of operations any further from where he worked.

I alternated between looking at the ground for footprints and eyeing the thick woods in the center of the valley. I moved slowly, concentrating on the search for clues. Whenever I came to a good observation post, I'd stop and surveil those woods, looking for movement. This area was not included in any of the hiking guides.

The chances of running across some random person were almost non-existent. It was a wildlife area, not a park. Hunting here was forbidden, and deer season was long gone. I suddenly began to worry about bears. This was an ideal habitat for them, and the winter's hibernation was over. We hadn't thought to bring bear spray, though we were both armed.

Gunshots would send our hermit into hiding and destroy any chance of finding him that day. Of course, then I started worrying about Brody. I'd sent a woman off into the wilderness by herself, and now I was second-guessing that decision. I sat on a fat rock and called her on the radio.

"Be aware of the possible presence of bears," I said. "I hadn't thought about that."

"Great," she said. "Fucking bears. I probably look like a nice little snack."

"It ain't gators or mosquitoes," I said. "At least we have our guns."

"Have you seen anything yet?" she asked.

"Nothing," I said.

"Me neither," she said. "Meet you at the bottom."

After our brief conversation, I sat still for a while, taking in the mountain scenery and appreciating nature.

There were no roses to stop and smell, but a multitude of other scents filled the crisp air. I took some slow deep breaths, drinking in the refreshment. My meditation was disturbed by the sound of some critter approaching. I kept still, waiting to see what it was. A gray fox came into view from higher up the hill. It saw me and stopped, smelling the air. It didn't seem too concerned with my presence, but it came no closer. I let it go about its merry way before standing and continuing downward.

I had seen no fox on our mountain, despite spending many hours in the woods. I didn't even realize they lived around here. Now I knew that there was at least one of them roaming the countryside, which made me wonder about wolves and coyotes and more dangerous canines. I knew that coyotes lived everywhere in the state, but I hadn't seen one of them either. I guessed that they exercised extreme caution around humans. They hadn't been given the adjective wily for no reason. I wished I had my rifle instead of the pistol I was carrying.

I found no trace of the hermit on the rest of my descent. Brody called on the radio to say she was waiting for me. I hung a left and moved towards the center of the valley, staying near the base of the hill we'd just come down. Within a few minutes, I spotted her. She had a wary stance, looking not only for me but for any of nature's predators.

"I'm glad you're here," she said. "I was starting to get freaked out. Thanks for the bear warning."

"I saw a fox up there," I said. "But no bears."

"We bring some spray next time," she said.

"Did you find anything?" I asked.

"Maybe," she said. "There's a hint of a trail through some tall grass back there."

"Deer maybe," I said. "Let's go take a look."

She led the way back a few hundred yards before pointing out what she'd seen. Sure enough, I could make out where someone, or something, had walked through a little clear meadow not too long ago.

"Look for deer tracks," I said. "Or moccasin imprints."

Whatever had pushed through the tall grass had barely disturbed it. It had taken a keen eye to notice. We tried to be gentle on our way through, so as not to leave evidence that we'd followed. I saw no deer tracks. Several times we stopped to investigate what may have been a footprint, but none of them were definitive. The grass acted as a cushion, keeping the foot from making much of an imprint in the earth underneath it. *Maybe* became the word of the day. The grass gave way to woods and rock. We didn't find any more potential prints.

We were at another crossroads. Which way did he go from here? I didn't want to split up again and neither did Brody. I asked her to sit down and be quiet. I did the same. I tried to listen and smell, letting the woods tell me what it knew. I looked at the trees, deciding which way I would go if I was the hermit. I remained still as a stone long enough for Brody to get impatient. She gave me a look. The woods were keeping a secret. They had nothing to tell me concerning the hermit's whereabouts.

"Okay," I said. "We've got a little time left. Let's poke around some more."

"Would have been a good time to have Red with us," she said. "If there's something to smell on that trail through the grass he'd be on it."

"I can bring him back tomorrow if it doesn't rain," I said. "It's worth a try, but if Red doesn't pick up a scent he'll become a handicap."

"Let him try," she said. "If he doesn't get onto something, bring him back to me. We don't have a deadline to find this guy."

"I don't want to drive him deeper into hiding," I said. "He's probably got a safe place for times of danger. Someplace impossible to find."

"Like Pop's cave?" she asked. "Because you found that."

"I did, didn't I?"

"Quit selling yourself short," she advised. "You're assigning superpowers to a vagrant. He's just a man."

We wandered around close to the wood's edge, looking for any sign of a man. We didn't find it, so we ventured a little further into the forest, staying within eyesight of each other. The underbrush got thicker and thicker. As we followed the path of least resistance, it funneled us to the banks of a small creek. There in the mud just above the water line, was a footprint. It had no tread marks, but it was clearly the mark of a shoe. I couldn't believe our luck. We'd walked for miles, finding only what might have been a path through the grass. This was solid evidence. The print seemed to match what we'd seen previously. We were on the right track. Our hermit was in the area.

Unfortunately, we'd found the print too late in the day. We had a good starting point for the next attempt. We were making progress. I made a waypoint on the GPS so we could take a direct route to that spot when we came back. We'd figure out where to park and how to get here later. I accepted Brody's suggestion to give Red a shot at it too. In spite of my doubts, we were closing in on the hermit.

We took a break to eat and drink before starting the long hike back. We didn't have to return the same way we'd come. Using the GPS, we took the most direct route possible to the car. We paused briefly as the sun went down over Roan Mountain, recalling the many sunsets we'd enjoyed in Florida. It was mostly dark before we got to the car, but now we knew how long it would take to hike back to that little stream.

"Our search area has been greatly reduced," Brody said. "Not a bad day's work."

"He's across that stream," I said. "And I'm betting not too far. It's a source of water for him."

"Not as hard as you thought," she said.

"We haven't found him yet," I said. "But we are narrowing it down. Thanks for your help."

"Other than the bear threat," she said. "I'm actually enjoying this."

"That's awesome," I said. "There's something special about being out here. I never dreamed I would like it so much."

"I'm starting to see it too," she said. "I took some time to appreciate my surroundings today. The scenery, the breathable air. It was nice."

"We'll turn you into a mountain woman yet," I said.

"Getting there," she said. "Trying to keep up with you."

Back at the cabin, we poured over the maps again, finding a place to enter the wilderness closer to that little stream. We had our waypoint on the GPS so we could make a beeline for it with Red in tow. I didn't know if dogs were allowed in the wildlife area, but so far we hadn't seen another human. I doubted it would be a problem. I gave him some of my steak after dinner to provide a little extra protein. It was time for him to join the team on this mission.

The SAT phone rang before we could leave the next morning. It was Rominger with news from Beech Mountain.

"The Chief has recused himself from the investigation," he said. "Says he can't participate."

"Why in the hell would that be?" I asked.

"The person who was in that house is his son," he said. "We have his fingerprints on file from a previous encounter. We swabbed him, and his DNA matches that taken from the beer can."

"What was he doing there?"

"He says he just stopped for a little private time before going home from the resort," he said. "He still lives with his parents."

"How old is he?"

"A grown-ass thirty years old," he said. "The homeowners say they never gave him a key and they didn't leave one hidden. The extra key was hanging on a hook just inside the door. It's there now."

"He could have swiped it and made a copy during an authorized visit," I suggested. "Knowing that these folks would be gone for long periods of time. How thoroughly has he been questioned?"

"We talked to him on the phone as soon as we identified him," he said. "But he's not at his folk's place. We haven't brought him in yet."

"Do you know where he is?"

"Working on it," he said.

"If he was innocent he'd be talking," I said. "Especially to his father."

"He might be talking to his dad," he said. "But the dad ain't talking to us."

"Can he do that?" I asked. "I mean legally."

"Technically, yes," he said. "But it certainly clouds his job future."

"You say there's a prior history with his son?"

"Minor troubles that have always been kept quiet," he said. "One of our guys got him on a DUI. Played it by the rules and booked the kid, but his punishment was nothing. Didn't even lose his license."

"He's not learned the consequences of his actions," I said.

"Seems to be a recurring theme with young people these days," he said. "He wasn't evil or anything, but he always seemed a bit off."

"How so?"

"Young men around here tend to drive pickup trucks, hunt deer, and chase girls," he said. "This one drives a Subaru, plays video games and doesn't have any friends."

"Didn't go to college?"

"Quit after his first year at App State," he said. "Works at a smoke shop in Boone."

"Not exactly making daddy proud," I said. "What's his name?"

"Zack," he said. "We've sent his photo out to all concerned."

"Has anyone from the resort confirmed that he was there during the night in question?"

"We haven't been back there to question anyone yet," he said.

"The staff would know," I said. "Bartenders, waitresses, even one of the Beech Mountain officers that might have been working security. Will they recuse themselves on the Chief's behalf?"

"They wouldn't care to lie to other law enforcement personnel," he said. "Regardless of how much they support their boss."

"You going to talk to them today?" I asked.

"Actually, no," he said. "Angelina Will is going up there. She's the closest thing to an investigator Avery County has. I think she can get people to talk, especially the males."

"No doubt," I said. "But I'll be steering clear. Brody and I have been working our way deep into the bush out west of town. We may be onto something."

"If Zack is our guy you're wasting your time," he said. "But that's on you."

"Not necessarily," I said. "He was very close to Buckeye Lake during just the right timeframe. Won't know if we don't find him."

"My people are going back to the house to look much closer," he said. "Our evidence people want a more thorough look. Blood residue, signs of a cleanup, anything attached to the girl."

"Good luck," I said. "Let me know what you find."

"You too," he said. "Keep us posted as well."

The involvement of the Chief's son was certainly a twist I hadn't seen coming. Learning that he'd experienced a certain privilege with law enforcement added a new dimension to the investigation. I knew a small town Chief when I was growing up that would ticket his mother if she was speeding, but I don't think that's the norm. What cop wouldn't go easy on his own kid, or at least pull a few strings for leniency?

That part of the riddle was out of my hands and wasn't my area of expertise anyway, although Brody probably had more experience than most of the actual cops on the case. We were relegated to the woods. That's where I could make a difference, assuming the hermit was somehow connected. Red was eager to give it a try, so we loaded him into the car and headed off for the Cherokee wilderness. We took bear spray with us this time, just in case.

When we let Red out of the car, he had to run around and shoot a bunch of trees before we could get started. New turf always had to be marked. He'd been cooped up for the most part lately and was eager to run, but we kept him reigned in until we got well away from the parking area. It was a long hike to where we'd left off, and we humans had to conserve our energy.

We used our GPS to find the creek with the footprint in the mud. I pointed it out to my hound dog. He didn't know what I was trying to tell him. I got down low and put his nose near the print. I made sniffing noises. He put his nose right down in the mud and checked it out.

He looked at me as if to say *Sorry, man, but no dice.* I motioned for him to circle the area and he dutifully obeyed. He tried, but there was no scent for him to follow.

"Take him back to the tall grass," Brody said. "Try over there."

I had him follow me to the faint trail that we'd found. He stopped twice along its length, investigating further with his nose, but didn't hit on anything definitive. We ran out of grass, made a U-turn, and tried again. He paused at those same two spots briefly but moved on without getting too interested. He'd caught a slight whiff, but not enough to go chasing after. I had no way to tell him that I needed him to track that tiny smell. I took him back to the print in the mud and tried to get him to make the connection. If he was a person, he would have shrugged his shoulders and said *okay, you're the boss, but it ain't enough to go on.* He tried anyway. I led him across the skinny creek to the other side, and he started to sniff around. It took him a good fifteen minutes, but he let me know he wanted to give it a shot.

"Go ahead, boy," I said. "Find him. Sniff him out."

He moved much slower than he normally did. His nose was almost touching the ground as he swung his head from side to side, trying to concentrate the faint smell he was working with. He clearly understood what I was asking of him, and was trying hard against tough odds. Brody and I had time to look around due to the slow pace. We each kept an eye out for other types of clues that would help with our search. What we were following wasn't so much a trail, but more a natural way of walking through the woods. It was now the easy route for anyone coming this way. The hermit had become less concerned about a tail at this point.

Maybe that's why we started finding more obvious footprints. They were widely scattered, but they told us that Red was going in the right direction. Brody and I whispered between ourselves, waiting for Red to grow more confident and take off with earnest after his target. It didn't happen. He wasn't getting a stronger scent. He wasn't any more positive of his direction. He kept his slow, nose-down pace and plodded ahead. It was nerve-wracking for us. We were obviously onto to something, but Red was reluctant. It wasn't a sure thing to him. I had no choice but to follow his lead. I'd brought the dog to do his job, I couldn't second-guess him now.

Then we came to a literal fork in the road. There were two obvious paths into thick cover. Red stopped.

He didn't know which path to take. I urged him on. He took the trail to the left for twenty or thirty yards but came back to the fork. He tried the other way. He came back again.

I'm sorry, I got nothing either way.

Ten

We each had bear spray and a weapon. We had our radios. We had to split up. I took Red further down the right-hand fork while Brody went to the left. At some points, the trail turned into a tunnel as the vegetation closed in over my head. It would be a good place to have a secret wilderness hideout. Finding it was another matter. I looked for a sign that would show me that the hermit had left the trail and dug deeper into the brush, but the path continued forward unbroken.

Red was constantly trying to regain the scent, but so far hadn't found it. The ceiling got lower and lower until I was forced to crawl. I sent Red in ahead of me. The low tunnel came to a dead-end. I couldn't understand it. The man had to have gone somewhere. He wouldn't create a dead-end just to throw off his pursuer, would he?

I called Brody on the radio to see if she was having better luck.

"The path has turned into a low tunnel," she reported. "I don't want to crawl in there."

"Same thing here," I said. "Ours is a dead-end."

"Bring the dog over here," she suggested.

"On our way," I answered.

Red and I backtracked to the fork and went in after Brody. We found her down on the ground, shining a small flashlight into the tunnel.

"It's just big enough for a person to crawl through," she said. "I can't see the other end of it."

Again, I sent Red ahead of me. I followed him on my hands and knees until we came to another dead-end. When we ran out of tunnel, Red was anxious. He whined and sniffed and turned in circles with his nose down.

"You got something, buddy?" I asked the dog.

He looked at me with a *maybe* expression.

"Sniff him out, boy," I said. "Find him."

My dog was determined, but he couldn't be sure he had the scent. He sniffed every square inch around the end of the tunnel before coming back towards me. He continued smelling the ground and the brush on either side. I watched, and waited until he disappeared into the undergrowth.

"He's after something," I told Brody. "I'm going in with him."

"Be careful, Breeze," she said. "Keep that radio on."

Between two groups of thick immovable branches was a void filled with tall weeds. The weeds acted as a curtain, disguising the entrance to a side tunnel. Red had the scent now, I was sure of it. Soon I was able to stand. Red gave me a single bark and slipped through another curtain. On the other side was an off-grid survivalist's dream camp. The dog was sniffing all over the place.

"Easy, boy," I told him. "You found it. Good boy."

We had found the camp but not the man. Red wanted to keep going, but I made him sit while I took a look around.

"Found a camp in here," I told Brody. "I can come back for you if you want."

"I didn't see where you went in," she said. "Come back for me."

I looked at Red and told him to stay.

"I'll be right back," I told him. "Sit still for me."

I crawled back through the double curtains to the tunnel and hailed Brody. She crawled towards me with her little light shining. She wasn't fond of spiders and snakes and looked none too pleased to be in this particular situation, but that didn't stop her. When we got back to the camp, Red was gone.

"Shit," I exclaimed.

"Why didn't you tie him up?" Brody asked.

"He hates that," I said. "I hate it too. I thought he'd stay for me, but I guess he couldn't resist chasing the scent."

"What do we do now?"

"Start processing this place," I said. "I'll get the dog."

I called him several times and listened for a response. I heard him bark and headed in that direction.

"Sit, stay," I yelled. "Stop."

He yelped again, and I got a better sense of where the sound was coming from. I plowed through the woods, ignoring the need for awareness. I wasn't particularly stealthy either. The need to recover my dog overrode other concerns.

"Where are you, Red?"

One last bark and I was able to find him. He sat obediently in a small clearing, waiting for me to catch up. As soon as I put the leash on him, he was ready to continue tracking. I wasn't so sure that was a good idea.

"Brody," I said into the radio. "I've got Red, and he's got the scent. What should we do?"

"There's a lot to look over here," she said. "I say follow it. I'll be okay here."

"Keep your eyes and ears open," I said. "Keep your weapon at the ready, just in case."

"I'm fine," she said. "Go ahead."

I was apprehensive about leaving her alone, but I wanted to follow the scent as much as Red did. He was happy to oblige. I let him loose and waved my hand in the air.

"Sniff him out, Boy," I said. "Go get him."

He already knew which way to go. He took off at a good clip, nose down and ears flopping. I had to hustle to keep up. This was a fresh scent, the best we'd found yet. I tried to regain my sense of awareness and caution as we went. I kept my eyes ahead of us and tried to hear more than the movements of my dog. I tried to gather clues from the woods.

I put together a theory in my mind. The hermit was at his hideout when he heard us coming. He probably heard us way back at the fork, or at least when we talked on the radio while searching the tunnels. It was plenty of time for him to gather a few things and take off. We'd been loud and maybe even a bit clumsy as we zeroed in on his location. It was not how I would have preferred to make my first encounter with the man, but without the dog, I'd have never found his camp.

Now he'd bugged out just ahead of us. This was his turf, and he likely knew it extremely well. Based on what we knew about him so far, he probably had plans for just this event, maybe even multiple options for escape. A dog was the only thing that could foil those plans now that he was on the run. I urged Red on.

"Let's go, boy," I said. "Get after him."

The dog was definitely onto something. All I could do was follow. He picked up speed, confident that he was on the trail. We were almost running when we encountered a rock wall. Its sheer face went straight up. There was no way I could climb it, and there was no way to get Red to the top. My dog barked at the rock wall, standing on his back legs with his paws on the stone. He looked up and continued barking. How had the hermit gone up? It seemed humanly impossible unless he was Spiderman, but Red was telling me that's where he went.

I walked around the right side of the edifice. A steep cliff dropped down to a creek. It wasn't much more passable than the rock face. I tried the left side. It looked passable, though difficult. I called for Red to follow and began carefully picking my way over and around rocks. The dog was dubious. I had to pick him up occasionally to bring him along with me. Meanwhile, the hermit had the opportunity to put more distance between him and us.

It took way too long to make it to the top of the rock wall. The hermit was long gone by then. Red picked up his scent, but it would be useless to continue. We didn't want to be out here after dark. We didn't have the necessary supplies, nor the will. We'd gotten close, but come up short. I found a rope tied to a thick tree at the top of the cliff. The hermit had set up his escape long before we'd ever been part of this chase. He simply pulled the rope up behind him before we got there. It wasn't an unexpected development. It went pretty much as I had figured it would. I knew what I had to do.

Brody and Red would not be involved. I had to come alone, ready to immerse myself in the woods. I'd known it from the start, but I needed a way to narrow the search. Brody and Red had helped me do just that, but in the end, they'd given us away. The hermit had been ready for this occasion. It hadn't been that hard to plan for, but would he be equally prepared for what I knew I was capable of? Were his skills better than mine? He had a knack for remaining unseen, but so did I. It was doubtful that he had any experience being tracked by a legit mountain man. I was eager now to test myself against him. All of my doubts and fears about this challenge evaporated. I wanted it.

Red was pissed when I called him off the search. He didn't like it one bit.

"Sorry, buddy," I said. "We've got to round up Brody and go home. Good job. Good boy."

I scratched his ears the way he liked, but he was having none of it.

I would have had him. I was right on his tail. Why are we stopping now?

I felt silly apologizing to a dog, especially since he was right, but I had Brody to consider.

"We're on the way back," I said over the radio.

"What did you find?" she asked.

"A clever escape," I said. "Red still had him, but we've got to get out of here before it's too late."

"Let me show you what I've found so far," she said.

I had to give Red a tug every now and then on our way back to the hermit's hideout. He figured I was going the wrong way. He was right, but there was nothing I could do about it now. I was happy to see Brody again. Her smile was much nicer than Red's frown.

"I've got DNA all over the place," she said. "Hair, nail clippings, you name it."

"What if he's not in any DNA database?"

"I can devise a makeshift fingerprint kit at home," she said. "It won't take but a minute to pull as many prints as we want."

"Assuming this is still here tomorrow," I said.

"You think he'll tear this whole thing down overnight?"

"I don't know," I admitted. "More likely he'll take what he wants and move on. Probably has a backup site out here somewhere."

"There's a treasure trove of information here," she said. "I'd hate to lose it."

"Do you want to come back tonight?" I asked. "It will be way dark by the time we can get back here."

"I don't think we have an option," she said. "I'll round up some Ziplocks, tweezer, and what I need to take fingerprints. Some good flashlights too."

"If you're game I'm game," I said. "Kind of exciting actually."

"The faster we get home, the faster we can get back."

"Let's roll."

We half-jogged during the trip back to the car. Red was still reluctant to leave. I had to spend a few minutes paying penance when we got home. He didn't turn his nose up at the food I offered as a peace offering, but instead of taking his place on the couch, he chose the rug in front of the fireplace to lie on.

Eleven

Brody dug out some good flashlights to add to our packs. We grabbed a quick bite to eat before driving back to the Cherokee Wildlife Management Area. We found a new parking place closer to the hermit's hideout. The GPS was hard to see at night, but we managed to follow it back to where we'd found the man's campsite.

We slowed and quieted on approach. I made Brody sit and wait while I listened for any signs of the hermit. I didn't think he was home, so we crawled into the tunnel towards his secret hiding place. I led the way through the double curtain of grass into the small clearing that featured a well-camouflaged canvas tent. It was an old school army surplus green model, covered in years of moss and fallen vegetation. It was impossible to see from the air, and almost invisible from the ground. It was pushed back into the thicket as far as possible. Outside were some obvious signs of occupation, including a pot and pan sitting on a grate over an open fire pit. Plastic storage containers lined one wall. There was a small woodpile, with a hatchet stuck in a tree stump.

We poked our heads inside and shined our lights around the interior. The bed was an inflatable mattress, covered with several decent looking comforters. Each sported bears or other cabin themes, likely stolen from Beech Mountain residences. There was a nice pair of boots next to the bed. A plastic shelf was full of paperback books. More plastic containers held clothes, dishes, and utensils.

"A lot more comfortable than Pop's cave," I said.

"I could almost live here," Brody responded. "If it had electricity and hot water."

"If he needs those things he walks up to Beech and takes what he needs," I said. "Or anything else that might come in handy."

It was a bit cluttered inside, but well-organized. There was a deck of cards on a small folding table next to the bed. An assortment of candles and battery powered lights were placed all around. A manual can opener sat on top of a stack of canned goods. Brody went to work collecting samples that would provide us with DNA. Once she was finished, she went outside and lit a small fire in the pit. She only let it burn for a few minutes before extinguishing it. She pulled a makeup brush out of her pocket and used it to collect some of the ash and carbon from the fire. She carefully carried the brush back inside and used the soot as fingerprint dust.

There were good prints visible on numerous surfaces. She used pieces of tape to preserve three solid prints and placed them in small Ziplock bags. If this man's prints or DNA were in any database, we had enough to identify him. We also had hair samples and even some fingernail clippings. All we needed was a match.

We had what we needed, but we continued to poke around out of curiosity. There was no sign of pornography or alcohol consumption. There was no bible amongst his library, nor anything else that would indicate interest in religion. There was no anti-government literature or post-apocalyptic novels. There was no hoard of silver coins, or any boxes full of cash. Other than the books and the playing cards, everything he stored in his tent were things needed for survival and comfort.

He had a modest collection of warm weather clothing. All of it was brand name merchandise, the type you'd expect to see in a cabin near a ski resort. Even the canned goods were a brand name. There wasn't a Walmart or discount brand among them. One of the plastic bins held assorted rice and pasta side dishes, the kind that come in foil pouches or bags. We found no weapons, no guns or a bow anywhere. We did find a good hunting knife, along with some twine and small branches that might be used to make a snare.

I perused his book collection, keeping in mind that they all probably came from houses on Beech Mountain. It consisted mostly of popular bestsellers but also included *Walden* by Henry David Thoreau. I found *On Golden Pond*, by Ernest Thompson, which I never knew was a book. I'd seen the movie many years earlier. There were a few books of local interest concerning the North Carolina Mountains, Appalachian Trail, and the mountains of North Carolina and Eastern Tennessee. All of these books were dog-eared and worn from use. I wondered if he ever dropped off the ones he'd read at the next house to replace whatever books he was taking. That was a common practice at marinas in Florida. I judged such places by the quality of their book exchange. I even started a few when my boat became overloaded with books.

All of the evidence before us indicated exactly what one would expect; a single man living in the wilderness. There were no earth-shattering discoveries of radical ideology or end of the world prophecies. He was just a guy, who for whatever reason, had decided to live in the woods and avoid society. I couldn't blame him, in fact, I sympathized with him. He was better off than the average homeless person. He lived close to nature. He had an endless supply of goods available to him close by, though he had to steal them. None of his victims were particularly harmed by his intrusions, which was key to his continued survival and anonymity. Too much heat would create an effort to hunt him down. He knew not to cross that line.

I questioned how he was able to gain access to these houses, so I started looking for tools. He had several different saws, a hammer with a collection of nails, and a canvas repair kit. Those weren't what I was looking for. I was searching for a lock picking kit, but didn't find it. He must have it with him, or it was stowed at another location. He was getting into those houses without doing them damage. He had to have a way to gain entry. Not finding such tools meant that he took them with him when he bugged out. He was probably sitting safely in a vacant property on Beech Mountain right now, freshly showered with a full belly.

I'd seen enough. Brody was done with her evidence collection, and it was getting late. We decided that we'd done enough and headed home. There was a different feel to the night on our way back to the car. We were full of excitement and anticipation on the way to the hermit's place. Now it was even darker, and an ominous feeling hung in the air. We couldn't move too fast in the darkness, and we couldn't see much. I felt vulnerable to predators, or even the hermit if he decided to retaliate.

"It's creepy out here at night," Brody said.

"I was just thinking the same thing," I admitted. "Ears open. Ready your weapon."

"Whose idea was it to come back out here tonight?" she asked.

"I'm pretty sure it was yours," I said.

"Should we sing or something?" she asked. "You know, to keep the wolves at bay?"

"If I could I would," I said. "But I'd be embarrassed for even you to hear my warbling."

"Warbling? What kind of word is that?"

"I thought it meant bad singing," I said.

"I think it's singing in general."

"Okay," I said. "My bad, out of tune, grating warbling."

"You have a nice voice," she said.

"Except I can't carry a tune," I said. "Trust me on this one."

"Keep talking then," she said. "Let the bears know we're passing through."

We kept the conversation going until we reached the car, hoping that it would somehow protect us from any wildlife that could do us harm. We vowed never to hike through strange woods again after dark. Both of us were relieved when we finally got back to the parking area.

"Too late to bother Rominger with our evidence," Brody said.

"We'll bring it to him tomorrow," I said. "That's quite enough for tonight."

I worried about another encounter with the sexy policewoman Angelina during the drive home. Rominger had called her back into the investigation at the ski resort. I hoped that our evidence collection wouldn't fall into her purview. Brody and I were as close as ever, but something about that woman made me weak in the knees. I didn't have a good history of resisting temptation. I recalled an incident when a Russian sex slave thanked me for my efforts. I had a girlfriend at the time. I didn't want to cheat on her, but the impromptu blowjob was more than I could resist. I let it happen, and I felt guilty about it later. I knew my weaknesses, and Angelina Will's charm fell right into that wheelhouse.

It had been an unusually long day. The sheer physical effort of the hiking caught up to me as soon as I sat down. Red came to nuzzle my hand, begging for a little rubbing. The next thing I knew it was almost morning. I woke up on the couch in an awkward position with Red at my feet. It wasn't daylight yet, and I was still exhausted, so after a visit to the bathroom, I joined Brody in bed. If I woke her, she didn't let on. Thankfully, I was able to fall asleep again in short order.

That's when the hermit showed up. It was just like an earlier dream. I'd catch a glimpse of him in the woods then he'd disappear. He was like a mirage, there but never within reach. He was always ten steps ahead of me, or ten trees, or ten rocks. I thought I had him twenty times, only to see him evaporate into the wilderness each time. Was he even there at all?

Something startled me in the night. Red heard it too. I slid silently out of bed and went to a window to look outside. Pop Sutton's face stared back at me. He had something to tell me. I wanted to open the window to get his advice, but it was still part of the dream. I was still in bed, and Red was snoring on the floor beside me. I gave up and got out of bed for real. I went straight to the coffee maker and turned it on. I put on some warm clothes and walked out on the porch to smell the fresh mountain air. The sun was starting to poke up over the mountains to our east. Rays of light shot through the trees like laser beams. One fat little bird pecked at our feeder, not afraid of my presence.

We hadn't eaten much the night before, and I was starving. I thought about cooking breakfast for a change. Brody always did the breakfast cooking, but I didn't want to wake her with the smell of bacon. I'd get on it as soon as she stirred. I crept around the kitchen as quietly as I could, drinking my coffee and taking bacon and eggs out of the fridge. I put bread in the toaster and butter on the counter to soften. There was no movement from the bedroom.

I took Red out for his morning constitutional. He chased four deer off the grassy area out back, but didn't follow them far. He knew better. They'd be back to taunt him another day, especially when the apples started falling off the trees. The creek was at a low babble due to lack of rain. The soft sound was mesmerizing, but the growling in my stomach was loud. I didn't let Red hang out too long. Once his business was complete, I made him come with me back inside. I peeked into the bedroom and saw that Brody was still out.

I couldn't take it any longer. I threw the bacon in the pan and scrambled some eggs in a bowl. I refreshed my coffee and put some bread in the toaster. The sizzling smells of breakfast stirred my gal, Brody. She staggered out in long johns and with her hair a mess. She was still beautiful. I handed her a cup of coffee and said good morning.
"Breakfast is my job," she said.
"Good morning, Glory," I said. "I thought I'd give you a break for once."
"God, I was sleeping so hard," she said. "When did you come to bed?"
"Three or four, I guess," I said. "Didn't look at the clock."
"I didn't have the heart to wake you," she said. "You and that couch were one entity."
"We're not teenagers anymore," I said.
"Speak for yourself, buster," she said. "Another cup of coffee and some breakfast and I'll be ready to do it all again."

"We need to take the evidence we collected to Rominger," I said. "No long hikes in the wilderness today."

"Oh, thank goodness," she said. "I'm quite beat."

"We'll take an easy day," I said. "The hermit is deep underground by now."

"How are we going to find him now?"

"I don't think it's a matter of we," I said.

"Time for mountain man Breeze to do his Zen thing?"

"Something like that," I said. "I dreamt that the hermit schooled me last night. He was literally a ghost."

"Just a dream," she said. "He's a man, like you."

"I also saw Pop Sutton in the window," I told her. "But he was part of the same dream."

"That's weird," she said. "A dream within a dream?"

"Remember American Werewolf in London?" I asked. "The guy thinks the dream is over. You think the dream is over. Then they scare the crap out of you, but it's still just a dream."

"That's pretty intense."

"That's why I've been up since the wee hours," I said. "Dying for some bacon. Sorry, I woke you."

"No, this is sweet," she said. "I'll go watch the creek while you cook."

I took her plate out to the porch before serving myself. I joined her with what was left of the coffee, refreshing her cup. We sat in silence for a few minutes, listening to the creek. There was a coolness in the air, but not enough to force us inside. Brody smiled at me with a twinkling eye. I smiled back but didn't speak. It was a nice moment. It was I who finally broke the silence.

"So what have we gained for our efforts yesterday?" I asked.

"Fingerprints and DNA are only useful if the suspect has been in the system for some reason," she explained. "If our hermit has never been arrested or otherwise tested for DNA, we won't be able to identify him, no matter how good our evidence."

"What's the likelihood he's in the system?"

"No way to tell," she said. "It's still a relatively new technology. It wasn't used in an American court until 1987. I'm not sure when law enforcement starting collecting it as a matter of routine, but if he encountered the police before then, he still wouldn't be in the database."

"How big is this database?"

"There are several all over the world," she said. "The first was started by Interpol. In the US, it's called CODIS. There are over ten million samples on record."

"So a person might be in the Interpol pool but not in CODIS?"

"Or any number of other national systems," she said. "It gets tricky when it becomes an international case."

"I don't think this will qualify," I said. "The hermit is local. He knows this area."

"He would have still had to have a run-in with the law," she said.

"We won't know until Rominger runs what we collected."

"Which is why we should get it to him as soon as possible," she said.

"Guess we're going to Boone," I said. "Ready when you are."

We cleaned up the dishes and gathered our evidence. We drove down the mountain to the headquarters of the North Carolina Highway Patrol. The dispatcher called Rominger in and offered us donuts while we waited. When our cop friend arrived, we greeted him with the evidence we'd collected.

"This is your hermit," Brody said. "Without a doubt. Great DNA and clear fingerprints."

"How in the hell did you get this?" he asked.

"We found his home base," I said. "Wasn't easy. We did not find him, though we were on his heels."

"That's freaking amazing," he said. "I would have never thought it."

"Oh yee of little faith," I said. "Never doubt Breeze, Brody, and Red."

"I'll send this to the lab right away," he said. "Son of a bitch. That hermit has been part of the local lore since I was a kid. Can't believe he's even real. Now we might be able to identify him."

"We want to know if you do," I said. "Immediately. We've invested a lot in this."

"You say you were on his heels?"

"We think he was at the camp but heard us coming," I explained. "Red had his scent but it got dark on us. Didn't want to risk continuing the chase. I was on his turf."

"If he did the girl, he could be violent," Rominger said.

"I've got no opinion on that yet," I said. "But we chose the cautious route."

"Can you find him again?"

"Seems to be the million dollar question," I said.

"If we can identify him, and depending who he turns out to be, we might be able to put you back on the payroll."

"I still can't say if he's connected to the girl," I said.

"Finding the Beech Mountain Hermit will be big news," he said. "A feather in the department's cap."

"More like Breeze's cap," Brody said. "Your department chose not to pursue the man."

"You're right," he said. "But it's got to go through us. We'll get all the credit."

"I'm okay with that," I said. "As long as you know who's really responsible."

"You'll be a legend with my men," he said. "Seriously. This is the biggest story to break around here in decades."

"If you can identify him," Brody said. "Remains to be seen."

We surrendered what we'd collected to Rominger's capable hands. We both trusted him. We weren't sure how the chain of custody laws would come into play if the hermit turned out to be our killer, but we'd done all we could on our end. The lawyers could figure that out later. My gut told me the hermit was not the killer, but that didn't dampen my zeal to pursue him. My subconscious kept telling me I couldn't catch him. I took that as a challenge. *Don't tell me no, damn it.*

We suffered a bit of a letdown during the drive home. What do we do now? It was much too late to chase a phantom in the woods. We were both too tired to go through that again anyway. We went back to the cabin and lounged the rest of the day away. I did spend some time going over the maps. We used the GPS waypoint that we'd made to mark the location of the hermit's homestead. Then we war-gamed surrounding areas for likely secondary hiding spots.

What we'd found was in the deepest, thickest part of the woods. The fact that we'd found it in the first place was amazing. The combination of skills that our little threesome possessed had been just right for the job. Now that he was flushed out of his hiding place, he might be even harder to find. Would he stay on the move, or would he simply retire to another hidden camp? The only way to find out was to comb those woods again. The dilemma was who would be involved. The dog had a skill that neither Brody nor I possessed, but he was a dead giveaway as to our location. Brody's critical thinking abilities were as good, or better than my own, but she wasn't the woodsman that I was. It all boiled down to me.

There was something otherworldly about how I could move about the woods. I didn't fully understand it myself, but I knew how to use it. It was becoming more and more apparent that I'd have to use those skills to their utmost if I wanted to meet the hermit. I couldn't say what would happen after that. I liked to think that I could sit down and have a chat with the man. That would be the most pleasing outcome for me, but I didn't have the final say. I told myself that if I could beat him in the woods, track him down and corner him, he would cooperate.

Twelve

I was no expert with topographic maps, but I noticed something during my study. It appeared to be a depression in a rocky area, like a bowl. I had to get Brody to assist me with the scale of the thing. We measured and re-measured until we were confident of its size. The diameter of the rough circle was ten feet, give or take. It was protected on all sides by solid rock. It looked like a great place to hide. We compared it to an aerial shot of the wilderness. The trees surrounding it were tall and thick. Their leaves and branches blocked any view of the ground below.

"That's where he went," I said. "A secondary camp for emergency situations. Probably has a cache of supplies there, and shelter."

"How far is it from the original camp?" she asked.

"Less than a mile," I answered. "But through rugged terrain."

"I'm no rock climber," she said.

"I'm not fond of it," I said. "But I thought I'd go alone anyway."

"Can you find it from the ground?" she asked. "Things look a whole lot different than on these maps."

"I'm going to sit here and figure it out," I said. "Get me the GPS."

Paper charts were old school, but I knew how to use them. I had enough data on the various maps to make a GPS waypoint dead on that depression in the rocks. All I had to do was walk to the waypoint. It would be accurate to within ten or twenty feet. It would be easy enough to find, but would he be there? If not, I'd have to go back to the drawing board.

I went to the garage and rounded up my stealth costume. The drab brown clothes hadn't been washed in many months. They were caked in old dirt. I shook them out and hung them on tree branches down by the creek. I left the deerskin shoes on a rock up the hill a little bit. I took a shower, but without soap or shampoo. I slept in the spare bedroom, so as not to pick up any scents from Brody. I was out of bed at four in the morning and hiking the woods well before daylight. I had the GPS to guide me. I had my dirty earthen clothes to cover my scent. I had my deerskin shoes to silence my footsteps.

I also had the ability to hear, see and smell at an elevated level. I had a feel for the woods. I could become one with the mountain. We'd been through this area a few times already. I had the GPS, but I almost didn't need it. *I'm coming for you, hermit.*

I went into full stealth mode right away. I slid through the trees like mist on a foggy morning. Once I was deeply immersed in the forest, I stopped to tune up my senses. I sat still and slowed my breathing, letting the sounds and smells come to me. I could feel my heart slowing down and the tension leaving my body. My eyes had become better accustomed to the dim light of early morning. I was ready to move on.

Each step was carefully placed to avoid making noise. I looked far ahead and up close at the same time. I used the trees and rocks for concealment, always assuming someone was there. I avoided detection by the imaginary foe with every move. My progress was slow and careful. I didn't want to announce that I was there, not even to the wildlife. I saw several animals on the move looking for breakfast. They didn't see me. They didn't smell me either. I was of the woods, undetectable even to the wary fox.

I saw deer and rabbits, along with a few squirrels. I didn't see any bears, though I had my spray at the ready. Not even the birds were alerted to my presence. I gained confidence with each animal encounter. If they didn't know I was there, then neither would the hermit. I thought about the rock depression I was looking for. He'd have to have a way to get down into it, maybe a ladder made from small trees, or just enough footholds to make the climb. I figured that if I showed up at the rim of the bowl, he'd be trapped. He couldn't climb out and get past me. He'd had an escape route at his other camp. Maybe he didn't have one at his backup spot. It would be his refuge of last resort.

If the rock depression was a bust, I would still have plenty of time to search the area. I could move like smoke all day if necessary. I was too close to give up if my first target came up empty. I could feel it in my gut. Today was the day. Yesterday's rest had me feeling strong. I was comfortable in my mountain man disguise, and my skin. I don't know why, but I was born to this. I must have had some mountain ancestors or something. Maybe it was in my blood all along, and I had never known. Now that I had discovered it, it seemed natural.

The sunrise was blocked by Beech Mountain. As daylight crept in, I increased my efforts to remain unseen and unheard. I felt I was barely moving, but continued making progress towards the hermit's suspected lair. I took a detour so that I'd be deeper in the woods and have more cover to use for concealment. The spring had brought green soft grass and weeds that didn't make a sound when stepped on. I kept up my sound discipline nonetheless. Any movement that caught my eye caused me to freeze behind a tree or rock until its identity could be determined, either through sight, sound, or smell.

There were no other humans in this part of the wilderness; that much I knew. The only person I expected to encounter was the Beech Mountain Hermit. He didn't know I was coming. He didn't know that I could find him. He didn't know that I could sneak right into his living room without him knowing I was there. I had to tell myself not to get overconfident. This dude hadn't survived anonymously for so long by being lax about his security. On the other hand, no one of my caliber had made an effort to hunt him down. Most folks weren't even sure if he was real.

I found a good hiding place to rest and let my guard down for a few minutes. I couldn't keep up my ultra-vigilance indefinitely, though I kept listening and smelling my surroundings. I took a minute to reminisce about the Hook Man of my youth. According to local legend, he lived deep in a forest that was popular with young couples. He attacked them while they were making out, using his steel hook hand to cause maximum damage. The story had floated around for several generations at least. Of course, no one ever saw the Hook Man, but somehow his legend persisted throughout the years.

Beech Mountain had its own legend, that of the Beech Mountain Hermit. The stories that circulated probably preceded the creation of the real thing. Some man, for whatever reasons, had turned himself into the myth. He'd dropped out and disappeared. He survived by the same methods that his mythical precursor had, breaking into houses and taking what he needed. It was an important part of the legend that he never did any harm. It made folks sympathetic towards him. During our search of the neighborhood he'd hit most often, we heard reports of people leaving things out for him to take so that he wouldn't break into their house.

It was a simple concept. If you were closing the place up for an extended period, just put a blanket and some canned goods out back. The hermit will accept your offering and leave your house alone. Some left books, warm socks, and even snacks, like cookies for Santa Claus. The real hermit had usurped the role of the mythical hermit and used it to his advantage.

A big part of me didn't want to take that away from the man. I had to give him credit. I almost admired him and his chosen path in life. It was a great big nose-thumb at society, something I'd done for many years in Florida. I couldn't see a way to get what I needed from him without exposing him. Everybody wanted to know who this man was. We'd already started that ball rolling by collecting his DNA and fingerprints. I wanted to find out what, if anything, he knew about the girl's death. I wanted to look into his eyes to see if he was lying, or telling the truth. I didn't know what I'd do if he said he knew nothing and hadn't seen anything. That was assuming I would be able to sit and talk with him. I'd find out soon enough.

I resumed sneaking through the woods like a ninja. I was the steam rising over a millpond on a warm spring day. I wasn't invisible in the true sense of the word, but I was as much a part of the scenery as a man could get. I made a slight detour to investigate the campsite we'd found. I doubted I would find him there, but it would be foolish not to check. I crawled slowly in the tall grass, listening for any sound of him. I filtered the scents in the air, trying to detect anything man-made. I knew he wasn't there, so I circled around the heavy thicket and took a more direct route towards the day's target.

I had to stop several times and consult the GPS. Brody was right about things looking different from the ground. The rock depression I was looking for was not visible to the casual passerby. It was well concealed by taller growth and rocks that appeared too difficult to climb. If this was his secondary dwelling, there had to be a way to get inside. I moved so slowly I thought that moss would start to grow on my skin, staying ever aware of the sounds and smells the mountain gave me.

That's when I smelled shit. No kidding, someone was pooping or had just finished the job. I knew he was in there, but how to get to him? I inched around the outside walls of rock until I saw some natural indentations that could be used for ladder rungs. A foot wide section was devoid of moss or other vegetation, worn down over time by the hermit climbing up and down. I checked it for trip wires or something that would alarm him of my approach and found nothing. I began my slow climb, remaining silent. I heard pooping sounds on my way up.

The thought of catching this guy while he was taking a shit was an unpleasant one, but it left him in a vulnerable position. Now was the best time to catch him by surprise. I increased my rate of climb ever so slightly. My soft shoes made no sound on the rocks. I reached the top edge of the bowl-shaped depression and peered down inside.

The hermit was sitting on a bucket, reading a book. He had not detected me. He was going about his business in what he thought was complete privacy. I took a quick look around. He'd created a nice homestead down in the bowl, complete with shelter, tools, and supplies. I was looking for a weapon but didn't see one. I was fairly convinced that this fellow was non-violent. The question was whether or not to interrupt him. I had located him at a most inconvenient moment for him. I had the drop on him, so to speak. It's tough to run with your pants down around your ankles, but he had no place to run anyway. He was boxed in.

"Good morning, mister," I said, without showing myself.

"You the man that found my camp the other day?" he asked. "You seem to have me over a barrel, or at least over a bucket."
"I am," I said. "Sorry to interrupt. The name's Breeze."
"How did you manage to sneak up on me like this?"
"I know a bit about the woods," I told him. "You want to finish up what you're doing? Maybe we can have a conversation."
"Some things can't be rushed," he responded. "Say your piece. What the hell are you doing hunting me down?"
"I'd rather wait," I said. "I'd like to come down and look you in the eye. I'll pass on shaking your hand for the moment."
"Other side of the rim," he said. "There's a rope ladder. Holds my weight."

I hadn't seen it. It blended in so well with the background that I'd missed it.
"Working my way around slowly," I said. "I mean no harm."
"Not much I could do about it if you did," he said.
I lost sight of him for a few seconds on my way around to the other side. When I saw him again, he had his pants pulled up. He set his bucket off in a corner and looked up for me. I found the ladder and hesitated before

climbing down. He would have me in a vulnerable spot as I descended.

"Okay, for me to come down?" I asked.

"It's what you came here for, isn't it?" he responded. "You went through all this trouble to find me; I may as well give you an audience."

His language and speech pattern was not that of a meth head or hillbilly. He was educated and intelligent. I'd seen no weapons or evidence that he'd try to hurt me. I had to trust that my gut was right. I climbed down the rope ladder to meet the Beech Mountain Hermit.

"Interesting attire," he said. "Part Davy Crockett and part I don't know what."

"Earth clothing," I said. "Smells like dirt, doesn't make noise."

"I never heard you coming," he said. "I'll give you that. When you had the dog and a lady with you, I heard from over a mile away. Didn't think you'd present a threat. Certainly didn't expect you to find me here."

"I need to ask you some questions if you don't mind."

"You some kind of reporter or something?" he asked. "Not interested in telling my story."

"About a girl's murder," I said. "She was found when the lake was drained. You were down there near the park at the time as far as I can tell."

"What are you?" he asked. "Some kind of Indian tracker? How would you know that?"

"I found your temporary layovers," I said. "My dog got onto you, but you disappeared into what would have been the lake."

"I take precautions," he said. "But here you are, to my surprise. I'd be curious as to how you did it, but I guess I'm more curious about your intentions now that you've cornered me."

"The girl," I said. "I'm trying to figure out who killed her."

"And I'm a suspect?"

"To some, maybe," I said. "My fault, I guess. I determined that you'd been in the area during the right time frame."

"That's unfortunate," he said. "But I didn't kill the girl."

"What did you see?"

I saw a change in his eyes. He knew something, but getting involved would mean jeopardizing his anonymity, and ultimately his lifestyle. He didn't want to tell me, but he knew it was the right thing to do. I let him wrestle with himself for several minutes.

"I'll make this as easy for you as I can," I said. "I'm not here to drag you back to society. I only want to find the girl's killer. If you can help in any small way, I'll do my best to leave you to your life."

"If it were only that simple," he said. "I was in the wrong place at the wrong time, after all these years. I didn't want to see what I saw. Now it's all going to fall to pieces."

"What did you see?"

"I haven't decided if I want to tell you," he said. "I'm afraid of what the future holds if I tell you anything at all."

"Which means that you know something," I said. "Let's talk about this. Maybe together we can figure out a way to catch the killer, without ruining your life."

"If I'm a witness, that ends it all for me," he said. "I'll be publicly identified. My mystique will be lost and I'll become a petty criminal. There's no romance in breaking and entering, my friend. Someone will want to put me in jail. I'd rather die as you might guess."

"What brought you out here in the first place?" I asked.

"No offense, but that's none of your business."

"I dropped out once," I told him. "Still not really a member of polite society. Look at me. You think I'm a stockbroker or a banker?"

"More like me than not," he said. "Finding me was an impressive feat. You're a man of the mountains."

"Wasn't always that way," I said. "I was a boat bum on the wrong side of the law most of the time. I had my reasons for shunning civil life, as I'm sure you do. I empathize with what you're doing out here. I'm not trying to end it. I'm trying to bring a killer to justice."

I tried to look beyond the beard and the dirt on the man. He was slightly smaller than me, but it was hard to determine his age. I thought he probably looked older than he was. Hard living does that to a man. If forced to guess, I'd say he was in his young sixties. He was fit and agile, still had his teeth, and showed no frailties. I felt bad for attempting to involve him in the case now. I had put his back up against a wall, almost literally. So far though, I was the only one who knew where he was. I still didn't know who he was.

I came right out and asked him.
"Who are you?" I said. "What drove you to this life?"
"That's a discussion for another day," he said. "If you care to have it."
"I'd be happy to come back if you'll have me," I said. "I think we may have a lot in common."
"I haven't carried on a conversation in many years," he said. "Can't really recall the last time."
"I'm sorry that it's under these circumstances," I said. "If I leave you today with no helpful information, you can

disappear as easily as you've done before. I've no desire to hunt you to the ends of the Earth."

"Tell me how I can help you without destroying my life," he said. "If you can do that, we'll talk some more."

Now it was my turn to wrestle with myself. I didn't have a good solution for him. In my zeal to find him, I'd dehumanized the man. I had a sense that this would end it for him, but I'd suppressed that in my mind. I'd been hell-bent on hunting him down to prove myself. It had been a selfish pursuit in that sense, but there was still the unsolved murder to consider. I had to weigh this man's freedom against bringing a killer to justice. My freedom was the most important aspect of my existence. Betraying him would be betraying my most basic instincts. I guess I hadn't thought this thing through.

"I'm no lawyer," I said. "But I want to be on your side. Can I have some time? Will you talk to me again? Give me a chance to think of something."

"I don't owe you a damn thing," he said. "But the fact that you tracked me down is worth something. Giving me a fair shake is worth something too. If you mean me no harm, I'll go back to my main camp. You can find me there most days. I'm good on provisions for now."

"Will you tell me your name?" I asked.

"If I'm right about you," he said. "You'll figure it out for yourself. Now I need to go dump my bucket if you don't mind."

"Meet you at the other camp?"

"Don't come if you can't solve the riddle," he said. "I'm not too old to disappear again, but I'll give you a chance."

"I can't ask for more than that," I said. "I'll be back in a few days. You think about what you want to do. I'll see if I can protect you, but if I can't, I'll still want your cooperation."

"Can't say you'll get it," he said. "See you in a couple of days."

Thirteen

I had looked the man directly in the eye. When he said that he hadn't killed the girl, I believed him. I was convinced though, that he'd seen something, either the murder itself or the dumping of her body. I understood his hesitation. Now I had to figure out a way to use what he'd seen without disclosing his identity. I didn't think that was possible. I'd bring a picture of the Chief's son back with me and let him decide how much he wanted to tell me.

I hoped to learn more about the hermit through the DNA and fingerprints that we'd collected. Maybe I could use that as leverage. I wondered how the investigation was coming along, relative to the Chief's son as well. I hoped that Rominger could help with both. I started the long walk back, checking the GPS and taking note of landmarks. I wouldn't have to sneak up on the hermit the next time unless he decided to run.

Now that I'd successfully completed my great quest to find him, and therefore validated my sense of worth as a mountain man, an anti-climactic feeling set in. He hadn't been that hard to find, and I was able to walk right up to the man without him detecting me. I had expected the hunt to be more challenging.

I turned my attention to other aspects of the case during the hike back to my car. I needed more information to put the pieces together. I needed to talk to Rominger, and most likely to Angelina as well. Dealing with humans was often much more difficult than dealing with nature. I didn't always express myself in ways that endeared me to others. Somehow I'd managed to become friends with Rominger, and Angelina seemed to like me well enough. I needed to suck it up and deal with both of them the best I could. I needed them if I was to be a part of solving the murder. They needed me if the hermit could, or would, help.

I ran it all past Brody after I got home. She helped me to take a step back and look at all sides of the situation. She was good at focusing on the big picture, whereas I tended to concentrate on the small details.

Together we could analyze the problem and work towards a solution.

"You caught him while he was taking a shit?" she asked, chuckling.

"Couldn't mistake that smell," I said. "I would have picked up on it from a mile away."

"Then you just sat and had a chat?"

"He said he didn't kill the girl," I said. "I believed him. I think he saw enough that he can help us solve the crime, but he's holding back."

"Because he doesn't want to be revealed," she said.

"Right," I said. "So how can we get his testimony without exposing him?"

"Written depositions are sometimes used in court," she said. "But he'd have to sign his true name to it. The defense would have to know his identity. You know, facing your accuser and all that."

"How credible will the word of a vagrant be in court?" I asked.

"They will attempt to use his status against him," she said. "They'll threaten him with charges on any number of offenses. They'll plaster his picture all over local media."

"We can't have that," I said. "That will be the end of him."

"I'll have to give it some thought," she said. "You don't think appealing to his sense of justice is enough?"

"I try to put myself in his shoes," I said. "Back when I was on the boat alone, and the law was after me, I probably wouldn't have come forward. It would have cost me my freedom."

"Not even to help catch a killer?"

"I didn't have a high opinion of law enforcement at the time," I said. "I was involved in too much bad shit to cooperate with the cops. I avoided them at all costs."

"What about our hermit?" she asked. "Other than petty theft, we have no reason to believe he's deeply criminal."

"We don't know," I said. "Maybe Rominger can fill in the blanks for us."

"You want to use the SAT phone to call him?"

"I assumed he'd call us as soon as he found out anything," I said.

"We'll check with him tomorrow then," she said. "Take another look at things once we're brought up to speed."

"You know that the pretty lady cop is working the Zack angle," I said.

"I trust you," she said. "I take it she has some investigative skills."

"I don't know if Rominger will be up to date on what she's been doing," I said. "I may have to talk to her. You're welcome to participate."

"We'll see," she said. "One step at a time."

We drove to Boone to visit the North Carolina Highway Patrol the next day. We were in no rush. We'd shared a nice breakfast and took care of a few chores before leaving for the day. There was no telling where our inquiries would lead us. We were greeted with gusto as soon as we entered the building. Several officers surrounded a table looking at pictures and newspaper clippings. Rominger saw me and waved me in.

"I was about to call you," he said. "We're still trying to put it all together, but we know the identity of the Beech Mountain Hermit."

"I met the man in person yesterday," I said. "But I still don't know who he is."

"Tyler Scott," he said. "Former CFO and Executive Vice President of Highlands Union Bank."

"Holy shit," I said. "How'd you hit on him?"

"Banner Elk PD picked him up for DUI after his wife's death," he said. "Fingerprints on file, not to mention an outstanding warrant."

"For what?"

"Failure to appear on the DUI charge," he said. "That's when he disappeared."

"What happened to his wife?"

"Car accident," he said.

"When was this?" asked Brody.

"2010," he said. "Mr. Scott took care of her affairs, attended the funeral, and vanished soon after."

"Left his money and properties behind?" I asked.

"His daughter had him declared dead last year sometime," he said. "She was the primary beneficiary of his estate."

"Was there ever any suspicion that he was the hermit?" Brody asked.

"None whatsoever," he said. "Bank executives don't tend to be wilderness types."

"No kidding," I said. "Where's the daughter now?"

"Here," he said. "Well, in Banner Elk. Living in a mansion in Linville Ridge."

"Her father's mansion?" Brody asked.

"That's the one."

"Have you told her that you think her dad is alive?" Brody asked.

"Not yet," he said. "This is just an hour old. We're still processing it."

"Heard anything from Angelina?" I asked.

"She located Zack," he said. "Brought him in for questioning and got nowhere."

"He's a free man?"

"Nothing to hold him on," he said. "He was on surveillance film from the resort, but not with the girl. Swears he never saw her. I don't have all the details."

"Do you have a picture of him?" Brody asked.

"Old mugshot is all we have here," he said. "Angelina is the one to ask."

"Can I ask you a favor?" I said to Rominger.

"Sure, shoot," he said.

"Can we keep this quiet for now?" I asked. "I think I can get the hermit to cooperate. I think he saw something. If we go plastering his story all over papers, he'll go silent. Most likely disappear forever."

"You do know this is the biggest story to break around here in a decade?"

"I realize that," I said. "But if this Zack kid is the killer, and Tyler Scott can identify him, then we can solve the girl's murder."

"Good point," he admitted. "I'll withhold it from the press, but some of these guys will talk about it to family and friends."

"Buy us some time," I said. "We'll go talk to Angelina and see what we can do."

"You can get in touch with the hermit again?" he asked. "How?"

"We have an agreement," I said. "I'll be visiting him again soon, but first I need all the information I can gather."

"We may need some kind of agreement not to hold him accountable for that warrant," Brody chimed in. "This can't be a setup to bring him in. Not if we want him to cooperate."

"The old warrant was returned to the Clerk of the Court years ago," he said. "I'm sure it still exists, but no one is actively working it. A decent lawyer could take care of it for him."

"Good to know," I said. "Think we can get the Beech Mountain PD to ignore the illegal entries?"

"As far as I know there is no evidence connecting him to the break-ins," he said. "No charges have ever been filed."

"We've got to learn more about the Chief's son," I said. "I'll get back to you on the rest."

"She's down in Newland today," he said. "At the Sheriff's office."

"Thanks," I said. "And thanks for the info."

"Least I could do," he said. "You gave us the evidence."

Brody and I discussed what we'd learned during the drive to Newland. The comparison between Tyler Scott and me was obvious. When my wife died suddenly, I'd snapped and dropped out of society. I chose a boat in

Florida instead of the mountainous wilderness, but the motivation was the same.

"I realize you didn't know the hermit's story," she said. "But you've had a soft spot for him from the beginning. It's a little bit eerie."

"I did sympathize with him," I said. "But I let my ego drive me to find him. I had to prove that I was better than him. I almost regret that now."

"He knows something that will help us solve a murder," she said. "You did the right thing."

"Imagine," I said. "Rich banker dude stealing canned goods to survive. Shitting in a bucket. Hasn't shaved in years. Probably wouldn't trade it for his old life at this point."

"Sounds like someone else I know," she said. "Would you go back to your old life given a chance?"

"No way in hell," I said. "Not even if you could come with me."

"What's that tell us about the man now?" she said. "How's he going to react?"

"He'll want to stay hidden," I said. "No doubt about it."

"So how do we entice him to cooperate?"

"We've got to give him a way out," I said. "Help him escape afterward if necessary."

"We don't have that kind of authority," she said. "We can't promise him anything."

"I don't need anyone's permission to help him," I countered. "To hell with the law. If he wants to roam free, I'll see that it happens."

"Why didn't I see that coming?" she said. "Aiding and abetting a fugitive won't help your relationship with the cops around here."

"Solving a murder will."

I was glad to have Brody with me when we pulled into the parking lot of the Avery County Sheriff's office. I hoped that Angelina would behave appropriately in her presence. I also hoped that any friction between the two women would be minimal. I wasn't up for a catfight. I tried not to show my hesitation as I held the door open for Brody to enter. The greetings were cordial enough. Angelina played it cool and welcomed us both into her office. Brody took charge right away.

"We know the identity of the Beech Mountain Hermit," Brody said. "Breeze has spoken to the man. Highway Patrol knows this information. Where are we with the Chief's son?"

"I'd be interested to know who our hermit is," Angelina said.

"Tell us about Zack first," Brody said.

"He's an impudent little prick," Angelina said. "If that was a crime he'd be behind bars, but I've got nothing to tie him to the dead girl."

"Lack of evidence," I said. "But what's your gut tell you?"

"I don't think he was evasive," she said. "He acted like my questions were beneath him, that the idea of him being involved was ludicrous."

"And you believed him?" Brody asked.

"Without any evidence, I had no choice," she said. "There was nothing at that cabin from the girl: no blood, no hairs, no nothing. Surveillance didn't put him with the girl at the resort. Staff didn't place him with her either. I wish things were different, but we've got nothing on him."

"How did he gain entry?" I asked.

"He was there with his parents at some point," she said. "Swiped a key on his way out. Came back as soon as the homeowners left and replaced it after he made himself a copy."

"Is there no criminal statute to cover that scenario?" I asked.

"Given the friendly nature of their relationship to the Chief, it's hardly a crime worth pursuing," she said. "I'll let the families hash that out."

"So we're all supposed to agree that his unauthorized entry into that house at the time of the murder is just a coincidence?" I asked.

"Evidence, Breeze," she said. "I've got to have evidence. Without that he's not a suspect at this time."

"What if I gave you a witness that saw him dumping the body?" I asked.

"Do you have such a witness?"

"I don't know, maybe," I said. "I believe our hermit saw something. He's reluctant to come forward. Do you have a decent picture of Zack I can show him?"

"We didn't book him," she said. "But he's all over social media."

"We don't have access to the internet," Brody said. "It's a Breeze thing."

"Let me look him up for you," Angelina said. "Just give me a minute."

I wasn't a total troglodyte when it came to the internet. I'd once used Facebook to find relatives of a Cuban girl I'd brought into the States illegally. She had family in Baltimore, which is where I eventually took her. Brody had been fully immersed in devices when we'd first met. Some bad actors had used that to track us, and I was nearly killed as a result. Since that incident, I'd forbidden use of the internet in our lives, unless it was an anonymous trip to the library. Too many eyes and ears were watching.

Within minutes Angelina had a Facebook profile and several gaming apps that showed clear pictures of Zack. She printed us out a few of the better ones and handed them to us. She asked if we wanted a copy of his driver's license, but I didn't think it was necessary.

"Given enough time, I can show you what websites he frequents, how much porn he watches, and what TV shows he likes," said Angelina.

"Too much information," I said. "Unless we can confirm that he's a suspect."

"I've been all over this guy," Angelina said. "I don't see him having what it takes to kill a girl."

"Maybe it was an accident," I said. "Without guts, he couldn't admit it."

"Bring me the evidence."

I had no evidence to bring her. I hoped that the hermit would identify Zack as the killer, or as the person who dumped her body. That was the only likely result. Otherwise we were chasing our tail. We said our polite goodbyes and promised to keep each other apprised to any new findings.

"She is beautiful," said Brody. "Seems damn smart too."

"Not as pretty or as smart as you," I said.

"I'm not so sure about that," Brody said. "She's younger than me, still working in the field. Makes me miss those days."

"How many times did you use your looks to your advantage while you were at the FBI?" I asked. "I'm not a woman, so I don't know how that works. Is it a big deal?"

"Knowing when it's appropriate is the thing," she said. "It works better with suspects than with fellow officers. It's still a man's club as far as I'm concerned. Women agents aren't taken seriously to this day."

"That doesn't sound like a modern government agency at all," I said. "Where's the political correctness and equal opportunity?"

"The FBI is outside normal government standards," she said. "Trust me on that. No female agent is going to expose harassment. Her career would be over."

"Were you ever harassed?"

"All the time," she said. "It's practically a rite of passage for women, but then I got involved with someone, and it stopped."

"Let's get back on topic," I said. "Miss Will says our boy Zack is not the killer. What do you think?"

"I didn't interview him," she answered. "But the woman seems competent. I can only take her word for it."

"If we eliminate the Chief's son then we have no suspects at all," I said.

"Ask the hermit," she replied. "That's all we have left."

We had one reluctant witness, and we didn't know what he'd seen. It was left to me to convince him to talk, but with no real incentive. He didn't know the dead girl. He likely didn't know who he'd seen by the lake that night. All I could do was take him the pictures of Zack and keep my fingers crossed. I could be his friend all day and make him promises with no end, but if he couldn't identify Zack as the killer, there was no point in exposing him. I was starting to lose hope. There was no way I'd get the hermit to come forward if the person he saw was not Zack. We'd be back to square one. I'd invested too much of myself in this mystery to give up, but I wouldn't know which way to turn if the hermit couldn't help.

Fourteen

The Beech Mountain Hermit was Tyler Scott, a former bank executive. His daughter had taken over his estate after having him declared dead. He'd dropped off the face of the Earth after his wife was killed in an auto accident. He lived in the wilderness now, but he made his way by taking what he needed from vacant seasonal homes in the resort area. His deeds were well known amongst the locals, who'd elevated him to mythical status in the embellished retellings of the story.

Even I had exaggerated the man in my mind. He wasn't quite the grizzled mountain survivalist that I'd imagined him to be. He had a crude, but serviceable shelter with enough amenities to keep him comfortable. His real skill was never being seen. He was more of a cat burglar than anything, sneaking around in the dark to collect his loot. He'd been wise to never steal anything of real value. What would he do with it anyway? Jewelry and other valuables were of no use to him. Anyone who owned a second home wouldn't miss a blanket, warm sweater, or some canned food.

As far as the girl's murder, we had no evidence whatsoever. The time her body had spent at the bottom of the lake had erased any clues. Zack's visit to the home of family friends didn't appear to have any connection to her death. It had only served to paralyze the Beech Mountain Police Chief from taking further action. The only thread we had left to pull was the hermit. Tyler Scott was our only hope. It was up to me to discover what he knew, if anything.

I thought about it for the rest of that day and into the night. The hermit had alluded to knowing something about the girl's death. There was no doubt that he could provide some piece of information about that night, physical description, car make and model, anything that we could work with. He could do that without actually being a witness, if we could use what he provided to find the killer, and garner some other corroborating evidence.

Then there was the ultimate question of justice. There was a killer out there someplace walking free. Someone had killed the girl and disposed of her body.

She didn't fall and bust her head and end up in that lake on her own. The notion of justice had to appeal to Tyler Scott. He wasn't born a hillbilly moonshiner with a hatred for cops. He'd been at the peak of society, a gentleman of some means. Certainly, he'd want her killer brought to justice.

I toyed with the idea of taking Brody and Red with me into the wilderness to talk to him, but dismissed it. This was all up to me. He might not want to talk in front of Brody. He might disappear when he saw or heard the dog coming. Nope, I was going back alone, armed with only some snapshots of Zach and a faint feeling of hope.

I'd found a closer place to park the car while studying the maps for the umpteenth time. I'd be covering new turf, but I felt that coming in from a new direction might be helpful. I wanted to stay one step ahead of the hermit at all times, just in case. I traveled light, carrying bear spray and my pistol along with a few bottles of water. I made good time by not concentrating on every small detail along the way. I had a goal in mind, and I worked steadily towards it. I didn't slow down and exercise much caution until I got close to his hidden lair.

I stopped and listened after crossing the grassy trail. Before entering the tunnel, I tried to pick up on any movement or smells from his camp. I hoped not to smell him taking a crap again. I started a slow crawl towards the hidden curtain concealing his hideout. I heard silverware on a cast iron pan. I smelled something cooking. He was cooking breakfast. I tried to distinguish the smell of his meal but couldn't place it. I crawled on, knowing that he was home.

I didn't want to startle him too bad, so before I poked my head through the last curtain, I announced my presence.

"It's Breeze," I said. "Permission to enter?"

"Come on in," he replied. "Didn't cook enough for two though."

"I've already eaten," I said. "But you go ahead."

"I marinated this squirrel all night long," he said. "Kind of looking forward to it."

"Marinated?"

"In a Ziplock bag so the bears wouldn't smell it," he said. "Nice Pinot Grigio from up on the mountain."

"Living large," I said. "I've only had squirrel fried, but that was a long time ago."

"Flour and breading won't keep out here," he said. "Can't waste the oil to deep fry. Mostly I saute. Swipe a stick of butter now and then if I've got something to cook. Otherwise, it's mostly cans."

"I ate out of cans for a solid year," I said. "Along with whatever fish I could catch."

"You fish up here?"

"This was in Florida," I told him. "After my wife died I disappeared into the mangroves to live in solitude."

He gave me an odd look, but didn't respond at first. He scratched his chin and thought about what I'd just told him.

"Did you make that up?" he asked. "Because I don't care to be trifled with."

"It's the God's honest truth," I said. "Something similar happened to you."

"So you know who I am," he said. "Or used to be."

"Tyler Scott," I said. "Banking big-wig, former man about town."

"How'd you figure it out?"

"We collected DNA and fingerprints the first time we were here," I said. "Your DUI gave you away. Still an outstanding warrant, by the way, but no one is looking for you."

"Except you," he said. "Doesn't matter who I used to be. That's all behind me now. It's long gone."

"I apologize for violating your privacy here," I said. "But I'm convinced you can help solve a murder."

"You certainly are resourceful," he said. "Who are you? You're not a cop. Private detective or something?"

"Just a guy," I said. "Trying to make up for my many misdeeds."

"Solving murders in your spare time?"

"Local law enforcement agencies use me as a tracker," I said. "Freelance sort of thing."

"Your skills are impressive," he said. "Either that or I've gotten careless."

"I've had mixed feelings about this," I said. "I understand freedom. I'm not overjoyed that I found you, but I do need your help."

"Freedom is the only thing I hold dear," he said. "It's all that I have, the only reason to remain alive."

"Trust me," I said. "I have a full personal understanding of what you're saying. I've lived it."

"Keep that in mind as we get further into this," he said. "Don't bullshit me on this. I'll make sure you never find me again."

I showed him the pictures of Zack. He took a good look and handed them back to me.

"Never seen him before," he said. "Not that I know many people these days."

"This isn't the man you saw that night?"

"Never said I saw anything," he said.

"But you did," I countered. "You saw something, or someone. Do you know who that person is?"

"No idea," he said. "I was hoping you'd bring me a picture that I'd recognize."

"Tell me what you saw."

"It's not going to do you any good," he said.

"Let me be the judge of that," I said. "A girl is dead. We've got nothing. You are the only one who knows anything at all about the crime. A killer is going to go free if you don't tell me what you saw."

He sat and reflected over his squirrel breakfast. It looked pretty good to me. He took a few bites and wiped his chin on his shirt sleeve before putting his pan down on a stump.

"I was down there close to the lake for the night," he said. "I had some stuff I'd gathered from the cabins. I heard the car pull in. It was past time for visitors. I got up and snuck down for a closer look. I wish I hadn't. I saw a white SUV, a small one, I think it was a Subaru. I got interested when he backed down close to the water's edge. It's soft down there so I thought he'd get stuck."

"Then what?"

"I got a good look at the man by the light inside when he opened the rear hatch," he continued. "He picked up what looked like a body. He didn't toss it overboard. He walked out into the lake until he was up to his chest in water. Then he pushed the body under."

"Was is wrapped up in anything?" I asked. "A rug, plastic bag or something?"

"Nothing," he said. "Just a body, fully clothed. Never got a good look at it, but I saw him just fine."

"Can you describe him?"

"Big but not fat," he said. "Buzz cut, square shoulders, maybe military. Had a stiff posture to him. Strong but not a bodybuilder. The weight was nothing to him. Lighter hair, could be blond or even reddish."

"Did you keep watching him after that?"

"I did," he said. "He left that hatch open the whole time. Got another good look at him when he got back to the car. He got in all soaking wet with muddy shoes. Drove off."

"You sure it was a Subaru?"

"Ninety percent sure," he said. "One of them Outbacks. I see them all over the mountain these days."

"Me too," I said. "Which means there's probably a hundred of them around here."

"Just telling you what I saw," he said.

"It's more than what I had," I said. "I'll relay it to the officers investigating the case. Maybe something will break."

"If it does, you'll come looking for me again," he said. "Have you told anyone where I am?"

"Only my gal, Brody knows," I said. "I did not tell the cops where you are. In fact, I got them to agree to keep your identity quiet for the time being."

"They agreed to that?"

"Only because they want to find the girl's killer," I said. "Word will get out eventually. People will know the true identity of the Beech Mountain Hermit."

"Had to happen sooner or later."

"Will it make a difference?" I asked. "So they know who you really are. Will that stop you from continuing to live your life as you have been?"

"Might send some more yahoos like you out here looking for me."

"I take offense," I said. "A yahoo I am not. I found you, but I doubt some yahoo could."

"Point taken," he said. "I'll have to give it some more consideration. If I can come out of this being left alone, that would be good."

"You're a dead man these days," I said. "Your daughter had you declared last year."

"Under different circumstances, I'd consider that a good thing," he said. "It was my ultimate goal."

"She's taken control of your estate," I said. "Living in your house."

"As it was meant to be," he said. "I only regret I couldn't transfer it to her sooner. Have you spoken to her? Is she doing well?"

"I have not," I said. "I assume that Highway Patrol will be in contact with her soon."

"She'll know that I'm still alive," he said. "Might cause her some legal difficulties."

"That's beyond my area of expertise," I said. "Maybe we can figure out how to make you dead again after this is all over."

"You are more invested in my future than you ought to be," he said. "What gives?"

"Freedom, brother," I said. "I told you that I understood."

"I'm starting to think that you do," he said. "Not sure why I should trust you, but I sense that you and I are kindred souls."

The last man of the mountains that I'd befriended ended up dead. I couldn't tell that to Tyler Scott. I didn't know what to say. I wanted him to trust me, but I couldn't promise that this mess wouldn't ruin his life, such as it was. I thought that most people would try to convince him to return to society, regain his station in life. I knew that was far from what he wanted.

"If we get a lead on this Subaru driver, will you make a positive ID for us?" I asked him.

"A visit to the police station will lead to a court appearance," he said. "I won't be testifying as Tyler Scott. I'll only be the Beech Mountain Hermit, ridiculed and embarrassed."

His reply illuminated a lightbulb in my head. An idea came to me, so I bounced it off of him.

"Why can't you testify as Tyler Scott?" I asked. "We'll clean you up and put you in a nice business suit. No one has to know who you are now."

"How do I explain my long absence?"

"Not relative to the murder case," I said. "Nor any of their business."

"You said the police used my fingerprints to identify me," he said. "Law enforcement already knows."

"I assume their highest priority is to take a killer off the street," I said.

"What about all my other crimes?"

"All good questions," I said. "We get an immunity deal in exchange for your testimony."

"You've thought this through," he said.

"It's been all I can think about," I told him, honestly. "I got involved in this case, and now I want to see it through. We started with nothing, but we're making progress. You are the key to this whole thing."

"I'm not making any promises," he said. "Keep working the case. Check back with me once you've gotten to the point that you need me. I feel like I owe it to the girl. Maybe I'll testify."

"I'll take that," I said.

"Find out about my daughter, please," he said. "Come tell me she's doing okay."

"Anything you want me to tell her?"

"I might be coming out of these woods soon," he said. "If so, it's best I tell her myself."

"Understood."

I'd gotten further with the man than I'd expected. I decided to leave while I was ahead. I wished him well and left him alone in the wilderness. Neither of us knew how much longer he'd be able to enjoy it.

Fifteen

While I was out in no man's land talking to a mountain hermit, wheels had been turning in the real world. Brody filled me in as soon as I got home.

"Word's out," she said. "Half of two counties knows that the hermit is Tyler Scott."

"Unavoidable I guess," I said. "Human nature."

"Here's the real kicker," she said. "The Beech Mountain Chief is seeking a warrant for his arrest."

"The hermit?"

"Yes, he's down at the courthouse right now with a stack of files," she said. "Rominger was here to warn us. Over thirty instances of breaking and entering and misdemeanor theft. I'm sure he's making a convincing case to a judge."

"The hermit knew this would happen," I said. "I didn't think it would happen so fast."

"My question is to the Chief's motives," she said. "What's the urgency? This has been going on for many years."

"He stood by and did nothing about a murder," I said. "Bringing in the hermit will make people forget about that."

"There's more to it," she said. "I don't like the way it smells."

"What is it?" I asked her. "His son? What are we missing?"

"I wish I knew," she said. "But something's up."

"I need to get what I've learned to someone," I said. "Rominger for one, but Angelina Will as well. Maybe they can tie a white Subaru to someone who fits the description."

"All the local agencies will need that information," she said. "But it's not up to us to dispense it. Let's go see Rominger."

Back to Boone we went. It seemed like we were wearing out the road between our cabin and the office of Highway Patrol. I felt all eyes upon us when we entered the building. One of Rominger's men directed us to an office in the back.

"Took about a minute for his name to be leaked," I said. "I could have used some more time."

"Did you talk to him?" asked Rominger.

"I got something good," I said. "But we can't bring him down here with warrants for his arrest."

"What did he tell you?"

"Why should I tell you?" I said. "I won't subject him to criminal prosecution."

"Get him a lawyer if you feel that strongly about it," he said. "But we're trying to solve a murder case here."

"He won't talk under duress," I said. "Plus you can't find him, no matter how hard you try."

"You could take us to him."

"I won't do it."

"What the fuck, Breeze," he said. "Don't you want to catch this killer?"

"None of the dozen or so police agencies around here has done a damn thing to find the killer," I said. "Brody and I are the only ones who have moved this case forward. Don't insult us like that now. I have another lead to follow. I'm happy to share it with you and everyone else, as long as the hermit doesn't have to worry about being arrested."

"We're not the ones asking for the warrant," he said. "You need to get this guy a lawyer, and his information will have to lead to the arrest of the murderer, or it's no good."

"Tell him what you know, Breeze," Brody said. "We'll leave here and find a lawyer. We need them to start looking for our suspect."

She was right, as usual. I realized how I'd made so many bad decisions in my life. I hadn't had her around to set me straight when I needed it. She knew just how to steer me in the right direction, and I was grateful for that.

"Here's the deal," I began. "Our hermit friend was down there by the lake the night of the murder. He heard a car come in way past normal visiting hours, so he investigated. He saw a white SUV, most likely a Subaru, back down to the lake. He saw a big man with a crew cut carry a body out into the lake. Not dumped, carried gently out into deeper water and submerged. The man returned to the car and got inside still wet and with muddy shoes. He got a decent look at him thanks to the car's interior light. He saw him going away and coming back. He can identify him if we get someone to show him. He doesn't know the person, but he says he doesn't know anyone these days."

"Any guesses to how many white Subarus are on the road around here?" asked Rominger.

"This one is connected to a big man, not fat or overly muscular," I said. "Military-like posture and haircut. It might have a severely muddy floor, or at least traces of the mud from the bottom of the lake."

"Gray muck it was," said Rominger. "Has some clay or something sticky in it."

"Find the car and the man," I said. "We'll have our killer."

"And you will bring the hermit in to testify?"

"Not without immunity," I said. "That's not negotiable."

"I'm not in any position to agree to that," he said. "That's for the DA to decide."

"District Attorney?" I asked. "For petty theft?"

"It's all about the murder now," he said. "Suddenly everyone is involved."

"Do they suspect our hermit?"

"I think that's the general consensus," he said. "His identity gets revealed as a result of the murder investigation. Easy jump for the average person to make."

"This is getting worse by the minute," I said. "He didn't kill the girl."

"How do you know his story isn't bullshit?" he asked. "A white Subaru has to be the single most popular car on the road around here. They're everywhere."

"I sat and talked with the man," I said. "I looked him in the eye. He's quite coherent. He used to run a bank for Christ's sake. He's no dummy, and he's no killer."

"Then bring him in," he said. "Get him to talk to us."

"First you have to find the suspect," I said. "Nothing will happen until then."

"If we weren't friends, I might take offense to how you give orders to law enforcement," he said. "But I understand. I'm on your side. I just want to put the killer away. I can't negotiate with you or the hermit. Get a lawyer. Talk to the DA. We'll look for this white Subaru."

"You'll alert all related agencies?" Brody said.

"Of course," he said. "We're going to have a lot of pissed off Subaru drivers very soon."

"Let us know when you get a lead," she said.

"I know that you were FBI," he said. "But leave this to us. We can't have you harassing the locals. Let us do our job."

"Sorry if I was telling you how to do your job," she said. "But we have no intention of stopping white SUV's."

"By the way," I said. "The hermit said he was ninety percent sure on the car make, not a hundred percent."

"Nothing like widening the search," he said. "But the driver is the key. Big guy with a crew cut."

"Right," I said. "Not fat, not overly muscular. Just big."

"Got it."

We left his office and got in the car. We realized we had no way to research lawyers in the area, so we drove to the library for some computer time. Brody found twenty-two criminal defense lawyers in Boone. I had some experience with defense lawyers myself, as a client. I became romantically involved with a hot redhead in Punta Gorda who got me a ridiculously light sentence for possession with intent to distribute. It didn't end well, but it was fun while it lasted.

I had paid another lawyer a ton of money to get me square with the IRS and to repay what I'd stolen from my employer. The court called it embezzlement, but whatever. The dual settlements cost me more than I'd cheated my employer and the IRS out of, but my freedom was the ultimate goal. It had cost me everything I had, but I was willing to pay it to be free.

We perused the internet directory of attorneys before deciding to question one Joshua Dorman of Dorman and Dorman. Brody had dug deep into the interwebs to discover his ability to effectively deal with the District Attorney's office on behalf of his clients. He sounded like our guy. Without a phone, we had no choice but to barge into his office and ask for an appointment.

The receptionist did her best to protect her employer from us, but Brody was too much for her. She got in the woman's face and backed her up while I snuck past and entered the lawyer's inner sanctum.

"Excuse me," I said. "I represent the Beech Mountain Hermit, and he needs your help."

"I have no idea what you're talking about," he said. "But maybe you can explain it to the police."

"I just left there," I said. "They told me we needed a lawyer."

"You're welcome to request an appointment," he said.

"I tell you what," I said. "I'll go ask your receptionist for an appointment ten minutes from now. You use that time to inquire with your contacts in law enforcement and the judiciary. Ask them about Tyler Scott, recently revealed as the Beech Mountain Hermit. I'll wait in the lobby, but only for ten minutes."

"Tyler Scott?"

"Highlands Union Bank," I said. "Formerly."

"Give me ten minutes."

I left him to his phone calls. Brody was still blocking the poor woman at the front desk from getting into the office of her boss. I asked her to stand down.

"He'll see us in a few minutes," I said. "You can put that in your appointment book if you like."

Brody and I sat down in the only two chairs available. There were two magazines on a small table. I grabbed the Golf Digest, though I didn't play the game. Brody was stuck with something called the Legal Management Magazine. We pretended to read until Dorman called us back into his office.

"A very interesting case may soon be before the court," he said. "Maybe two cases. I'd like to be a part of this, assuming the necessary funds are available."

"I'll pay for Mr. Scott's representation," I said. "Consider it covered."

"Let me recap what I just learned," he said. "Fill me in where necessary. As part of the hunt for the girl's killer, the Beech Mountain Hermit was somehow implicated. You volunteered to find him. The son of the police chief was shortly a suspect as well, but no evidence has been found to tie him to the girl. The Chief goes for warrants within minutes of finding out the identity of the hermit. Said hermit has provided information, through you, to law enforcement that may aid in identifying the killer."

"Accurate so far," I said. "News runs through the police departments faster than juicy gossip at a woman's club."

"We feel like the Chief is more concerned about arresting the hermit than he is about finding the killer," Brody said. "Something feels odd to us about his priorities."

"Mr. Scott won't present himself to a court if he is threatened with arrest," I said. "We need to get him an immunity deal, or he won't talk."

"You were wise to come to me," he said. "Did someone recommend our firm?"

"Just some quick research at the library," Brody said. "Not much above pulling a name out of the phone book."

"I have an excellent relationship with all the county judges," he said. "Not to mention the District Attorney and his assistants. This type of work is my specialty."

"It's our lucky day, Joshua Dorman," I said. "What do we need to do first?"

"Other than a financial commitment, nothing yet," he said. "I'll need to initiate talks with the proper people and see where it goes. Meanwhile, we don't have a murderer to prosecute just yet. Your friend can save his breath if the killer isn't found and arrested."

"Good point," I said. "The police didn't get his description until two hours ago."

"Anything else to go on?"

"A white Subaru," I said.

"I drive a white Subaru."

"Not big enough and no crew cut," I told him. "You're off the hook. I figured you for a Mercedes or a Lexus."

"These mountain roads are too tough on a luxury car," he said. "I lease my Subaru. Beat the shit out of them for two years and take them back for a new one. Company expense, of course."

"As many of them are on the road here, it's still small towns and communities," I said. "The police will narrow it down."

"In the meantime, I suggest the hermit stay underground," he said. "Don't let him talk to anyone, especially the police. Make sure he knows not to speak without me present."

"I'll pass it along when I can," I said. "I'm going to leave him alone until the killer is off the street. For his safety."

"The police may have been loose-lipped," he said. "But it will take a while for the news to filter out to the general public. Our killer may not hear about the hermit's true identity."

"Unless he's a cop," I said, just then making the connection. "Described as having a military posture. Crew cut. Big but not fat. Fit but not obviously muscular."

"Does that sound like someone you know?"

"The Beech Mountain Chief of Police," I said. "Just hit me."

"You reported feeling something odd about him," he said.

"He's been squirrelly since we discovered the house his son was in," Brody said. "Breeze and I canvassed the homes in the area that had not suffered a break-in by the hermit."

"But there was no evidence," he said. "Or so I've been told."

"The Chief stepped aside from the investigation," I said. "An Avery County Sheriff's Deputy took it over. She found the kid and questioned him, as well as going back to the house. She told me herself that there wasn't anything she could use to make the connection."

"It smells funny anyway," Brody said. "Too many coincidences."

"It's not my job to worry about the killer's prosecution," he said. "I'm here to keep Mr. Scott out of jail, and in turn securing his testimony when the time comes."

"That's what we're after," I said. "I think we have an understanding."

"How can I get in touch with you?" he asked.

"You can't," I said. "We'll check in as necessary."

He handed each of us his business card, encouraging us to call at any time. He was on the phone before we could get out of his office. Brody and I smiled at the receptionist and wished her a nice day. I suspected she'd be more cordial on our next visit. It was late, we were hungry, and there was nothing left for us to do that day. We drove back to our little creekside cabin to hide from the world for the night.

Red was at the door with his legs crossed. Poor boy, I'd forgotten about him in all the excitement. I let him run loose in the yard while I checked for signs of a doggie accident. There were none, so I went back outside to play for a while.

Sixteen

I couldn't sit still the next day. There was a manhunt going on, and I wasn't part of it. Brody sensed my restlessness.

"You want to drive around looking for white Subarus?" she asked. "Follow them to work or home?"

"The cops are better suited for that," I said. "What can I do though?"

"If we had a cell phone we could call the particulars and find out what's going on," she responded. "But I know I won't get anywhere with that suggestion."

"I'll take it under advisement," I said. "Maybe I will take a drive. Talk to the cops."

"Is Miss Will still involved?" she asked.

"I have no idea," I said. "She was handed the case on Beech Mountain, but I don't know if the kid is even still a suspect."

"Go find out," she offered.

"You're telling me to go talk to the pretty lady cop?"

"I'm not worried about her," she said. "If that's what you're getting at. I'm worried about you pacing around here like a caged animal. I've got shit to do. Go ahead. Talk to whoever you want."

"You're welcome to come with me," I said.

"I need a break," she said. "I'm not quite the Avenger that you are."

"I know we came here to get away from it all," I said. "I know I've promised you better."

"Breeze is Breeze, and that's the way it will always be," she said. "I can deal with that."

"Reason ten thousand why I love you so much," I said.

"You better."

I drove up to the top of the driveway and paused. I could turn right towards Boone, and find Rominger, or I could turn left towards Newland and Angelina Will. We'd been in Boone yesterday, I told myself. The decision to turn left was made. During the thirty minute drive to Newland, I told myself to turn around at least ten times, but the trip continued. Even after I was in the parking lot of the Sheriff's office, I gave myself one more chance to leave and not go inside. I walked inside anyway.

The dispatcher told me Angelina was on the road. I presumed she was checking out white Subaru. I asked if she could relay a message.
"Deputy Will, there is a Meade Breeze here to see you."
"I'm not near the shop," Angelina replied. "Ask him to meet me at 111 Morning Song in twenty minutes."
"I don't have a phone or GPS," I told the dispatcher.
She told Angelina to stand by while she showed me on a map. I jotted down some quick directions and thanked her.
"He's on his way," the dispatcher said.

The address was a private residence. There was a Sheriff's car in the driveway. Before I could ring the doorbell, Angelina opened the door.
"Welcome to my home, Breeze," she said. "Come on in."
The little devil on my left shoulder and the little angel on my right shoulder began a furious argument. So many times in my life, I knew I was about to do something wrong but did it anyway. This was one of those times. That realization did not stop me from entering the home of Angelina Will.

She was on me as soon as the door closed. She kissed me passionately, and I returned the sentiment. It was not a one-sided affair. The kissing continued long enough to evolve into roaming hands. She tasted like champagne and smelled like heaven. Breeze junior was wide awake and ready for action. She could feel my readiness poking her and trying to bust out of my pants. Her hands moved to undo the button at the top of my jeans.

This had always been the point of no return for me. Desire became too great to change my mind once things had gone this far. I suffered from a condition that had only one cure. I was too weak to deny myself, even when I knew that I should. I found the strength that I needed as Angelina began to unbutton her blouse. I put my hands on her shoulders and very gently pushed her to arm's length. I looked at her beautiful face, felt her inviting body, and said no.

"I can't do this."

"You know you want to," she said.

"I'm not arguing that," I said. "But I can't."

"Because of Brody?" she asked.

"I love her," I said. "Maybe it seems old-fashioned, but I can't betray her."

"That's impressive willpower," she said. "Now I want you even more."

"Please," I said. "Stop before my willpower fails. I'm begging you. You're so hot and desirable, I can't believe I'm saying no. I do want you, but I just can't."

"Okay, I'm going to give you good guy credit," she said. "But why come here looking for me?"

It took me a few seconds to remember. The blood had left my brain several minutes prior.
"White Subaru," I said. "Big guy with a crew cut."
"Let me get you some water," she said. "You're not going to believe what I'm about to tell you."
I sat down and tried to pull myself together. I was embarrassed, but Angelina had given me a reprieve. She left me alone long enough to return to normal. For that I was grateful. She came back and handed me a bottle of water. I couldn't interpret her smile. I was afraid that if she reinitiated contact, I'd have no defense. I'd used up my strength already. I tried to forget how pretty she was, and conjured an image of Brody's equally pretty face.
"The Chief's wife owns a white Subaru," she said. "Zack drives it often. The Chief himself matches the description you gave to Highway Patrol."
"That's enlightening," I said. "I made that realization about the Chief yesterday."
"You told a lawyer, and he told some cops and so on and so on," she said. "Now the Chief himself is a suspect."
"Have you searched the car?"
"We haven't found the car," she said. "Zack left in it yesterday afternoon, soon after all this news broke."

"APB?"

"If he's on the road he'll be found," she said. "A little tougher if he's holed up somewhere."

"The Chief?"

"Lawyered up and not talking," she said. "Not under arrest either. We have to examine that car."

"So who's the killer?" I asked. "The Chief or his son?"

"It always comes down to evidence," she said. "Or a confession."

"You're a good cop," I told her. "You'll figure it out."

"And you're a good man," she said. "I'm sorry about earlier. I misread things. Please accept my apologies."

"It's not your fault," I said. "I knew what I was walking into."

"I hope that Brody knows what she has in you," she said.

"I'm the lucky one," I said. "I thank God for her on a regular basis. On that note, I'd appreciate it if we could avoid any further incidents like this. No offense intended."

"Probably for the best," she said.

"You should go find that car," I told her. "You being the cop and all."

"Yep," she said. "Let's get out of here."

"Thanks for letting me off the hook," I said.

"You've almost restored my faith in men," she said. "But only almost."

"Men are dogs," I said. "Don't forget it."
"Most of them."

The further I got from her house, the clearer my thoughts became. It was evident that the Chief and his son were involved in the girl's death. The son was on the run in the vehicle that the cops had been looking for. The father had clammed up. I needed to get a picture of the Chief to the hermit, preferably a full-body shot. Maybe a picture of the car too once it was located. The son did not match the description. He didn't seem to have any of his father's traits. I didn't know what the mother looked like, but I had to assume the boy favored his mom.

I tabled that train of thought for future consideration. I moved on to chastising myself for going to see Angelina. I'd felt a strange excitement during the drive to Newland. I'd ignored all the warning signs and driven through the metaphorical stop signs. I wanted to see her. I was drawn to her like a moth to the flame. I knew that sleeping with her would destroy my relationship with Brody. I was aware that it would ruin the life we'd forged together, even if Brody never found out. I would know. Things would never be the same, but that didn't stop me from going. I'd let it go too far, but finally came to my senses. Having put a stop to the festivities allowed me to forgive myself. It had taken more strength to say no at that point than it would have taken not to go at all. I'd stared down my greatest temptation. I held it, kissed it, felt its electricity, and was able to say no. I knew this was all a grand rationalization, the truth was that I'd fucked up royally, only saving my sorry ass at the last possible moment. I needed a way to call that a win. I also needed to get back home to Brody.

My last thoughts as I turned onto Pigeon Roost Road were all about Brody. I made a solemn promise to myself to never let anything like today's events happen again. How many times can you taste the ice cream before you go ahead and eat the whole bowl? I wondered how a supposedly smart guy could sometimes be so damn stupid. It wasn't the first time that I had tried to solve that riddle. I gave myself a sharp rap on the noggin before going in to talk to my girl.

She had a funny smile on her face when I came in, like she knew something was up. Her eyes twinkled like they did during special moments. She gave me a kiss that was more than the standard welcome home greeting.
"How did it go?" she asked. "Did you talk to the hot cop?"

"I did," I admitted. "It was frustrating, in more ways than one."

"You want to tell me about it?"

"Well, the Chief's wife drives a white Subaru," I began. "The boy took off in it as soon as he heard what was going on. We need that car, but it sure looks like Father and son are part of the murder at this point."

"All well and good," she said. "But I'm more concerned about the rest of it."

I knew better than to lie to her. We'd grown too close. She could practically read my mind. I wasn't a great liar to begin with.

"She came on to me, hard," I said. "It's okay if you connect frustration with hard. That's how bad it was."

"I see," she said. "How did you respond?"

"I'll be honest with you," I said. "I hesitated ever so slightly. She took me by surprise, and I can't say it wasn't pleasant, but I put a stop to it. Nothing happened."

"How did she take it?"

"Graciously," I said. "Believe it or not. I think we reached an understanding."

"I think I'll have to consider this an act of supreme gallantry," Brody said, taking my hand and pulling me towards the bedroom. "Let Nurse Brody relieve your frustrations and soothe your wounded soul. Let me reinforce just why you turned the pretty lady down."

I tried to please her in return, but it was all about me. In spite of my obvious foolishness, I was being rewarded for doing the right thing in the end. I was being reminded just what I had in such a valuable partner. It was a lesson well-learned, and much appreciated. I can't say that it was well-deserved, but it was one that would stick with me for the rest of my days. Most women would have been pissed off and enraged with jealousy. Brody knew better. She sensed it before I confessed any of it. Her trust in me had been justified, and our love had been solidified beyond a doubt.

I was mentally, physically, and perhaps even spiritually, blown away by the way Brody had handled the situation. I struggled to say something appropriate.
"You're an amazing woman," was all I could come up with.
"I think we've reached our own understanding, wouldn't you say?"
"Absolutely," I replied.

Seventeen

The entire Highway Patrol of North Carolina was on the lookout for the car and its driver, as was every county sheriff's department and local police force. Short of looking for the car ourselves, there wasn't much that Brody and I could do to help the cause. I spent one day at home taking care of chores and playing with Red, before I felt the urge to do something. We drove down to Boone to talk to Joshua Dorman.

He seemed like a well-connected guy, so we hoped he had some inside information for us. We didn't have an appointment so we had to sit and wait for thirty minutes before he could see us. We made small talk with the receptionist, who was now our best friend. Finally, Joshua opened his door and waved us in.
"You seem to have created a real hornet's nest," he said. "Every bit of the buzz is about this case."

"Let's just hope it all works out for the best," I said. "What's with the search for the car and the kid?"

"All hands are on deck," he said. "He has to be in hiding. Law enforcement is reaching out to everyone he's ever known to try to find him. His mother has checked herself into a mental health facility and isn't talking. His father has been suspended from active duty. He's still not talking."

"What does the court say about our immunity request?" Brody asked.

"General feeling is that we'll get that approved," he said. "We still need an arrest, and then we'll see who gets the case. Convicting a Sheriff of murder is a much bigger deal than arresting a vagrant for petty theft."

"Especially if that vagrant is the star witness," I said. "The only witness."

"Assuming he ID's the Chief," he said.

"I hadn't considered any other possibilities," I said. "If he doesn't then we're screwed. There is no case."

"There's a lot of circumstantial stuff now that the son has disappeared," he said. "The Chief's lack of cooperation speaks volumes as well. The prosecutor's office will break them and get to the bottom of it, if one of them is guilty."

"Solid evidence sure would be nice," I said. "Mud in that car. Muddy shoes. Blood or hair."

"The police only have the girl's body," he said. "Which was washed clean of that type of evidence. They don't even have a crime scene."

"I'd look for it, but I don't know where to start," I said. "We scoured every likely address on Beech Mountain."

"Maybe something was overlooked," he said. "The initial investigation never really got off the ground, right? Except for you two."

"That's right," I said. "The Beech Boys didn't have a clue how to proceed. The Chief was happy to delegate the property search to us."

"The Chief and Officer Sally are the ones who gave us the list of properties to search," Brody said. "All the Chief had to do was leave off the real crime scene."

"Maybe Sally was not complicit," he said. "He just didn't know."

"Of course not," I said. "He gave all of his information to the Chief. It wouldn't take much to alter the list. Erase one and reprint it or whatever. I think we were sent on a goose chase."

"That seems like something you could work on," he said. "If you can get the necessary cooperation."

"If I can't, I know people who can," I said. "You've been helpful, thanks."

"I'm here to serve," he said. "Have you been in touch with Tyler Scott?"

"I have not," I said. "Get me some pictures of the Chief, and I'll take them to him. I need a good full body image."
"I'm sure I can arrange that," he said.
"Then we just wait for the car and the kid to be found," Brody said. "The waiting is the hardest part."
"I'll get Rominger up to Beech Mountain PD," I said. "Try to take another look at those properties. It will give us something to do in the meantime."
"Give me a day to get some pictures," he said. "I'll leave them at the front desk for you."
"Great, thanks," I said.

Brody and I got in the car and headed to the office of Highway Patrol. As long as we were moving, I felt like I was doing something to help. Brody welcomed the chance to return to the search for clues on Beech Mountain. Rominger put a little kink in our plans right away.
"Deputy Will has the Beech Mountain assignment," he said. "You'll have to ask her."
Brody and I looked at each other and shrugged.
"So be it," she said. "I guess we'll drive down to Newland."
"I can call ahead if you want," Rominger said. "Maybe save you the trouble."

"No, we'll go see her in person," Brody said. "Not much else to do today."

So there I was, driving in the car with my lover and best friend, to go speak with the sexy woman who'd just tried to seduce me, and almost succeeded. It was uncomfortable, to say the least. I tuned into No Shoes Radio and listened to Kenny Chesney tell me he was learning how to build a better boat. I still had an attachment to boats and beaches, but I hadn't looked back much on those times. We'd built a better life here in the mountains, with apologies to Kenny Chesney. I hoped that when this mission was over, I could learn to sit back and enjoy it more, instead of chasing murderers and hermits all over the wilderness.

We soon learned that Angelina was out chasing down leads. I asked the dispatcher to let her know that Breeze and Brody would like to meet with her. I put a little extra emphasis on "and Brody." Angelina radioed back that she was on Beech Mountain. We said that we'd meet her at the police station up there. Brody reminded me for the fourteenth time how much easier life would be with a cellphone. She was obviously correct, but I hated the things. I had a not so irrational fear of loss of privacy, and I didn't want to be tracked. I didn't want law enforcement, the government, or Google, to know where I was and what I was doing every second of the day.

I grew up and entered the workforce in the ancient times before smartphones. How did we ever survive? We had no internet. We had no home computers. We all lived in caves apparently. We'd tried owning all the devices once. Our troubles with the law were over. Neither of us was wanted by the FBI. Brody fell right back into her old habits, always connected, always showing how awesomely useful these devices could be. It almost cost me my life. Bad actors tracked us, or at least our internet searches. They ambushed us at a place we would never expect to be found.

A giant of a man broke my body in multiple ways before Brody shot him. As soon as we figured out how we'd been found, we ditched the devices. I didn't wish to rejoin the modern fascination with being connected. Brody understood that, but she'd be much more immersed in that than I was. I'd never signed up in the first place. It was easier for me to go without.

Angelina was waiting for us inside the Chief's office. She stood to greet us both with a pleasant smile.
"Let's keep this professional, shall we," Brody said.

"Of course," Angelina replied. "What can I do for you?"

"We're rethinking the crime scene," I said. "Or the lack of one. We think the Chief may have jiggered with our search list to protect himself, or his son."

"What was the basis for that list anyway?" Angelina asked.

"Originally, the hermit was a suspect," I said. "We ruled out the homes that we knew he'd entered. He never struck the same place twice."

"For starters, he's no longer a suspect based on what you've told us," she said. "Second, there are a thousand houses up here that haven't been broken into. I'm not sure why or how we'd want to tackle that."

"We've got three intelligent people here," Brody said. "Where was the girl killed? How do we find it so we can collect some hard evidence?"

A silence fell over the room. We all sat in contemplation, rethinking everything we'd previously thought about the case. This went on for ten minutes or more. The silence grew eerie. I spoke more to end it than to add to the investigation.

"We know she was at the Beech Mountain Ski Resort," I said. "We know the son was at the house Brody and I found. Maybe it happened somewhere in between, but maybe not. The father was the one seen dumping the body. Let's try to make some sense of this."

"We can't place the girl with the son at the ski lodge," Angelina said. "If she left alone, anything could have happened."

"Where was the Chief?" Brody asked.

"Here in this very office," Angelina answered. "According to him."

"Where do they live?" I asked.

"Here on the mountain," she said. "We've been to their house, but not with a full forensics team."

"How hard did you look?" Brody asked.

"I wasn't a part of that effort," Angelina said. "They live on the Watauga County side."

"Highway Patrol wasn't involved either?" I asked.

"Unfortunately, no," she said. "None of us have an abundance of resources."

"Consider Brody and I as additional resources," I said. "Get us permission to crawl all over that place."

"Do you know how hard it is to reopen a warrant after the fact?" Angelina asked. "The judge will say he already gave us permission once."

"He gave the Watauga County Sheriff's Department permission," Brody said. "We go somewhere else. Get a warrant for Highway Patrol."

"Same judge," Angelina said. "We could try Avery County, but they'll question the jurisdiction."

"Someone left this investigation to you," Brody said. "At least the Beech Mountain portion of it. Tell them you're following the trail and you need to get on that property and into that house."

"It's worth a shot," she said. "Watauga County won't like it. It will make them look bad."

"That can't be our concern," Brody said. "We're trying to solve a murder."

"I'll bother a judge in the morning," Angelina said. "What else are we missing?"

I got up and went to the big map on the wall. I removed all the pins that we'd placed previously. I put one red pin in the center of the ski village. I put another at the park beside Buckeye Lake.

"What's the Chief's address?" I asked.

Angelina used her phone to pull it up. She came over and stuck a pin on the Chief's property.

"Somewhere within this triangle, or damn close to it, the girl was killed," I said.

"We can't walk the whole area looking for blood spatter," Angelina said.

"It's a start," I said. "A thought process. The ski resort, the Chief's house, and the lake. What went down?"

"The kid killed the girl," Brody said. "He drove the body home to daddy. Dad disposes of it."

"That simple?" Angelina asked.

"Think about it," Brody said. "Your son shows up at your door with a body in the car. You're the Chief of Police. No one is in a better position to protect their child. What do you do?"

"I'd like to think I'd do the right thing by the law," Angelina said. "But I see your point. That's a tough call for a parent."

"How's the house the kid was in come into play?" I asked.

"The father takes him there to clean himself up," Brody said. "Then sweeps the place clean. Figures we'll never find it. No one will be the wiser."

"So he didn't alter the list?" Angelina asked.

"We're wargaming right now," Brody said. "Try to keep up. Feel free to jump in at any time."

"We did hit that house pretty well," Angelina said. "We got the fingerprints and the beer can, but no signs of blood or hair."

"The body was never in that house," Brody said. "It was in the car the whole time, at least until dad took it to the lake."

"He tells his son to clean up while he disposes of the body," I suggested. "Comes back and picks him up afterward."

"The car was at that house, and also at the Chief's house," Angelina said. "We need to take a look at those driveways. Doubtful we could still recover anything lakeside. It's been too long."

"We have to assume that the Chief will have a good understanding of how to best cover his tracks," Brody said. "But blood is virtually impossible to make disappear completely. Modern techniques can find it, bleached or not."

"The car is the answer," Angelina said. "We've got to find it."

"What are your leads?" I asked.

"Slim," she said. "He didn't have many friends. No relatives in the area."

"Do you think his parents know where he is?" Brody asked.

"Seems likely," she said. "But we can't touch the mother, and the Chief is mute. If he covered up a murder committed by his kid, why would he turn on him now?"

"Will he go to jail in his place?" I asked. "That's what it's going to come down to."

"I don't have an answer for that," Angelina said. "It would be an interesting thing to research."

"We'll leave that to you," I said. "Or the prosecutor."

"Where's this all leave us?" Brody asked. "What do we do now?"

"I'll try to get another warrant for the Chief's house," Angelina said. "You're welcome to comb the grounds of the ski resort. Maybe find some blood in the parking lot next to Subaru tracks. Miracles happen."

"About as likely as finding clues down at the lake at this point," I said. "But that girl was killed somewhere. There is a crime scene."

"Let me know when you find it," she said.

Angelina's phone rang. She indicated that it was Rominger as she put him on speaker.

"Is Breeze there with you?" he asked.

"Yes, both Breeze and Brody," she answered. "We're on Beech."

"We spoke with Tyler Scott's daughter," he said. "She's desperate to get a message to her father."

"Go ahead," Angelina said. "We can all hear you."

"She says for him to come home," he said. "He's welcome to take it all back."

"Nice family sentiment," I said. "But I don't think he cares about that stuff anymore."

"She needs him to know," he said. "She didn't know he was alive. She didn't know what else to do."

"I'm working on getting some pictures of the Chief for the hermit to identify," I said. "Once I have those, I'll go talk to him."

"You could have asked me," he said. "I'm sure we can come up with something. There's always the internet."

"Breeze is internet phobic," Brody said. "You should know that by now."

"A real throwback," Rominger said. "I don't know how you two do it."

"Like everyone did it for thousands of years," I said. "It's not so hard."

"We promised we'd get this message delivered," he said. "Send it in smoke signals if you have to. Just tell him what she said."

"I'll take care of it."

We'd run out of things to discuss for the time being, so Brody and I thanked Miss Will for her time and left Beech Mountain. Neither woman had chosen to be catty, which suited me just fine, but Brody was able to subtly insert her superiority over the other woman. I assumed that made her happy, but I'd learned long ago never to think you've figured women out. Most importantly, I'd come out of the confrontation unscathed. My hide was intact, and I still had Brody. I couldn't ask for anything more, considering my behavior.

Instead of heading down the mountain, I drove to the ski resort. I pulled into the upper parking lot, which was empty this time of year, at least during the day. It was a vast gravel area with no painted lines. Visitors parked every which way during the season. I stopped close to the village and turned off the car.

"What are we going to do here?" Brody asked.

"Look around," I said. "Stumble onto the crime scene."

"Really?"

"You never know," I said. "Won't hurt to walk the grounds."

"Where do we even start?"

"The village is on this level," I said. "There's the brewery and the lodge. We can rule out the common areas where someone would see the murder. Look at the lights. Find a dark area out of sight from other visitors. I know the cameras didn't catch them leaving together, but let's say she was out here on her own. The kid finds her and comes onto her or whatever. It doesn't go well, and he bonks her on the head. He's got to get her into the car. It could have happened around here someplace."

"Big ass parking lot," she said.

"Which is now empty of cars," I responded. "Dried blood or whatever."

"Ridiculous longshot," she said. "Too much time has passed."

"I'm open to other options," I said.

"Let's get looking."

Eighteen

As soon as we got out of the car, I realized how ridiculous this idea was. It would take a week just to cover the parking lots. I tried to picture Zack dragging a body from the resort area out to his car. That didn't happen. If the murder occurred at the resort, it had to be close to the parking lot, or in it. There were three lots, all equally large and daunting. We were at the highest level. "You want to split up?" I asked Brody. "We each take a lot and meet at the lower one."

"Okay," she said. "But don't waste a lot of time. Just cover ground and keep your eyes open."

"I'll go down one level," I said. "Meet you at the bottom."

As I walked downhill to the middle lot, I noticed a small strip of grass, trees, and shrubs separating the two levels. The open gravel areas had some minimal lighting, but this bit of vegetation did not. There was no need for the resort guests to walk there. I decided to start searching this natural barrier instead of the gravel. Again I tried to picture how the murder may have happened. If Zack's car was near this strip, he could ambush her from the bushes and get her into the rear hatch without being seen.

Why would he attack the girl? Was rape the motive? Maybe he hit her too hard. He wanted to assault her sexually but killed her in the process. What was the girl doing here alone? It was a good walk to her parent's rental cabin, but not too far for a fit teenager. She'd stayed late at the lodge, maybe trying to make friends, sneak some booze, or hookup with a boy. She'd left on her own, only to be clobbered in the parking lot.

This sort of thing simply didn't happen on Beech Mountain. The girl and her parents would have thought it a perfectly safe thing to do. I'd never met the Chief's son, so I had no way to form an opinion of him. I was also jumping to a bunch of conclusions. What I needed was evidence to back up our guesses. I kept looking until Brody came down from the upper lot.
"I thought we were searching the gravel," she said.
"New plan," I responded, explaining my reasoning to her.

"Makes sense," she said. "I'll go start on the next level."

The growth between the lots consisted of waist-high bushes and some scraggly trees. It was not great cover for a full-grown man, but it would be dark at night. The girl had no reason to be wary of attackers. The scenario I'd created in my mind seemed plausible, so I continued to search. I was starting to think that the search was in vain, when Brody yelled from down the hill.

She stood over a splotch of something. We couldn't be sure it was blood. There wasn't a lot of it, but there was a congealed black smear on the ground just at the edge of the lowest parking lot. We had no forensic tools to take a sample. The amount of time that had passed likely made collecting it useless in court, but it was what we were looking for.

"We've got to get the cops to come take a sample of this," Brody said. "If it matches the girl we're on to something."

"Look here," I said. "Squint your eyes and imagine her feet dragging towards the gravel."

"Could be," she said. "Check nearby for more blood."

We didn't even know if it was blood. Maybe someone puked up their booze on the way to their car, but we searched anyway. We found a drop here and a spot there of the same stain on the rocks close by. It was beginning to look like we'd found the scene of the crime. The Chief may have done a dandy job of covering up evidence to protect his son, but he hadn't known about this. The dead girl was delivered to his house. At least that's what we thought had happened. Sooner or later, all of the little pieces would come together.

"Go tell Angelina Will to send a tech up here," Brody said. "I'll keep looking and keep an eye on the scene."

"You sure you want me to go by myself?" I asked. "I can wait while you go."

"Drop it, Breeze," she said. "She gave it her best shot and failed. I told you I'm not worried about her. Should I be?"

"No, you should not," I said. "I'm a dumbass sometimes, but I'm not a complete moron."

"Don't be so hard on yourself," she said. "That girl is damn sexy. She's younger than me and just as pretty as she can be. I understand, but you did the right thing. You didn't break our bond. I've got to give you credit for that. You should give yourself a little credit too."

"I've lost count of the number of reasons why I love you," I said. "But there's another one."

"This is serious," she said. "Go get us a tech up here."

I left Brody standing guard over our mystery stains. There was no one to intrude, but she seemed determined to stay behind. I drove to the cop shop, half hoping that Angelina had left. She hadn't. I went inside with no idea how she'd react or what she might have to say. She smiled when she saw me come in.

"You made the right choice," she said. "Brody is the woman for you. I'm relieved that she didn't go off on me."

"I'm relieved that she didn't go off on me," I said. "I sort of confessed to our little encounter."

"What did she say?"

"She took me to bed and fucked my brains out," I told her.

"Smart move," she said. "She really loves you."

"Anyhoo," I said. "We think we found some blood over at the resort. We need an evidence tech pronto."

"No shit?" she asked. "After all this time?"

"Maybe," I said. "We won't know until we get it checked out."

"Stand by," she said. "I'll make the call."

I perused the big map on the wall while she was on the phone. The Beech Triangle stood out prominently, from the resort to the Chief's house to the lake. The chain of events seemed clear. When Angelina hung up, I went over the possible series of events in order.

"He whacks her here," I said, pointing to the resort. "He drives her home to daddy. Daddy drives her to the lake. End of story."

"That's all well and good," she said. "But we can't prove a single piece of it."

"Not yet," I said. "It starts with the blood we just found. Get that car, and you've got another piece. The hermit ID's the Chief dumping the body, and all three pins are covered. The Beech Mountain Triangle."

"What were you before you moved here?" she asked.

"A boat bum," I told her. "Beachcomber and fisherman."

"Forgive me for having a hard time believing that," she said. "But the tech is on his way from Boone. Let's go back to the resort and see what you've found."

"Thanks for being a good sport about all of this," I said. "It could have gone much differently."

"You're not completely innocent," she said. "But I won't pit myself against Brody. Someday I hope to be the woman that she is."

"I hope to be the man that she deserves," I said. "It's a work in progress."

"Come on, boat bum," she said. "We've got work to do."

We beat the tech to the resort by ten minutes. The first few minutes were spent pointing out the possible blood stains. The rest of the time was spent in awkward silence. All three of us had already spoken our piece about recent events. All three of us had decided to leave well enough alone. The arrival of the evidence tech was a welcome sight.

Brody and I left Angelina and the tech to their work. We'd contributed enough for one day. These people were getting paid to do their jobs. Brody and I had volunteered to help solve a murder. So far we'd been the only ones to advance the case. We'd found the house that the Chief's son had entered without permission. We'd tracked down the hermit, who was a witness. We'd found blood at the ski resort, or at least we thought it was blood. I was beginning to warm to the idea of setting up our own private detective business. We didn't have the tools that law enforcement had, but we had a knack for deep investigation. We also had plenty of time on our hands.

The hard part was constantly waiting on official law enforcement to carrying through with their duties. The white Subaru still hadn't been found. No one was doing much else as far as evidence collection. The Chief had been handled with kid gloves. He knew what went down, but no one was putting the screws to the man to make him talk. They needed evidence, but they weren't looking hard enough for it.

I'd run out of ways to contribute, other than being a liaison for the hermit. I was supposed to deliver him a message from his daughter. I was supposed to show him pictures of the Chief. I needed to step back from looking for evidence and visit Tyler Scott, but I was tired. I needed a day of rest. I needed to pay attention to my dog. I needed to pay attention to Brody. This mission had pulled me in too many different directions. I'd kept up with the pace, but I couldn't keep it up indefinitely. I needed a break.

"I'm thinking we need a lay day, if that's okay with you," I said to Brody.

"Things are about to break," she said. "I was thinking about concentrating on that car."

"I was thinking we lay in bed till noon," I said. "Go to Hickerman's for a late breakfast. Then spend the afternoon in bed too."

"I like your idea better," she said. "But only one day. We've got to see this through."

"I've got to go back to the hermit," I said. "We've got to pick up pictures from the lawyer first. Lots to do, but it can wait a day. Give me a good night's sleep, and I can start to repay you for the other night."

"I like the sound of that," she said.

We ate a decent meal and turned in early. I was asleep before I hit the bed. Red was curled up on the rug at the door. He wanted to be with us, but he knew he wasn't allowed in the bedroom. I was content in our little cabin. I had a wonderful woman and a faithful dog. I was hidden away from the world. I could hide from everything here, except for my dreams.

They came at me in rapid-fire succession. In the first dream, I saw the hermit down by the lake. I watched as he picked up a rock and smashed the girl in the back of the head. Then he disappeared into the darkness. Everything faded to black.

Then I saw the Chief at the house we'd investigated. This time it was him who killed the girl. In the third dream, it was the Chief's son, but he wasn't in the parking lot at the ski resort. He was outside that same house. I saw him and the girl climbing the steps. She slipped and went down, landing at the foot of the steps on her head. It had all been an accident, but Zack panicked. I waited for the Chief to arrive, but the dream faded.

I was awake. What message was my subconscious trying to send me? I did my best to slip out of bed without waking Brody, but I failed. She was a light sleeper like me. Always somehow alert, even when asleep. It was a habit I feared we would never break.

"What is it?" she asked. "Are you okay?"

"I'm fine," I answered. "Not nightmares this time."

"What's going on?"

"I just dreamt every possible scenario except the one we've chosen," I said. "The hermit did it. The Chief did it, or it was an accident."

"It could have been an accident," she said. "But why the cover-up? Why would the kid run? Why would the Chief clam up?"

"They were just dreams," I said. "But they make me question what we think we know."

"Shit, I'm wide awake now," she said. "You want coffee."

"Sure, babe," I said. "Sorry to wake you."

It took Red a minute to realize that we were up and about. He yawned and stretched before joining us in the kitchen. He sat by my side and asked for an ear rub. I scratched his head absent-mindedly while Brody poured the coffee.

"Is this a crisis of confidence?" she asked. "Or is there something eating at you about this case?"

"I'm not sure," I said. "How much faith do you place in dreams? Do they mean anything at all?"

"In your case," she said. "They've always been about the past. Old shit coming back to haunt you."

"True enough," I said. "But I've pretty much gotten over all that. I'm nightmare free these days. I've dreamt about poor old Pop Sutton more than once. I've seen the hermit in my dreams. Now I've got the Chief and his son joining the party."

"Getting a little crowded in that head of yours," she said. "Save some room for me and Red."

"They're dreams," I said. "Nothing to do with you. Believe me, I'd much rather see you in my dreams."

"Well, it's three in the morning," she said. "We've got no TV and no computer. Let's sit here and work this thing through again. Tell me what we've missed. Give me alternative choices. How else could the girl's death have happened?"

I warmed my hands on the mug and thought about it. I kept asking myself "what if?" What if the hermit is full of shit and making the whole damn thing up?" If he killed the girl, claiming to witness someone else commit the crime would be a natural self-defense mechanism. But why would he kill her in the first place? Nope, didn't make sense. If the Chief killed the girl, why would he take obvious steps to protect his son? Why would the son take off? Nope, that didn't make sense either.

"We need to find that car," Brody said. "Get a trace of the girl's blood or other DNA evidence that would confirm the body was in there. If that happens, then we know it was the kid or the father. No doubt about it. The lawyers will flush it out after that."

"I can't imagine any reason that a small town Chief of Police would kill a teenage tourist," I said. "It's not plausible."

"That leaves the son," she said. "Just like we've been thinking all along."

"Stupid dreams," I said. "Seems like tonight was all for nothing."

"Not necessarily," she said. "You seem rested enough."

"Are you thinking what I think you are?"

"No pressure," she said. "But this seems like a nice time for you to pay up."

"Gladly."

Just before I fell asleep, I remembered thinking that I probably still owed her, at least a little bit. I'd done a worthy job of showing my gratitude, but it had been my weakness that started this sexual chain of events. I vowed to be more of an unselfish lover until the Angelina episode was erased from our memories. It was a small price to pay.

In spite of the split sleep session, I felt better the next morning. We were ready to drive to Boone and get pictures for the hermit to look at and see what else was new. Joshua Dorman had a small portfolio prepared for us that showed the Chief from multiple angles and distances. He'd even found a photo of the car on Facebook, something I hadn't thought of.

"What's the latest scuttlebutt?" I asked him.

"The kid has already been convicted in the court of public opinion," he said. "It's just a matter of time until they find him."

"What if he refuses to confess?"

"The father will face pressure like he's never known," he said. "Once your man identifies him as the body dumper, he'll be screwed. He can take the fall himself, or rat out his child."

"What if he won't give up the kid?"

"He'll go away for a very long time," Dorman said. "Cops don't fare well in prison."

"I wouldn't want to be in his shoes," I said. "What if the son claims it was an accident?"

"If the evidence is overwhelming, he should do just that," he said. "But fleeing hurts his defense. He could have come forward from the start if it was an accident, especially with the counsel of his father, a law enforcement officer."

"Where is the mother in all of this?" Brody asked.

"The story is that she's had a complete breakdown," Dorman said. "The court would think twice about trusting any testimony she may provide. Law enforcement would likewise be hesitant to question her."

"So she's off-limits?" Brody asked. "She's in the thick of it. She has to know what happened."

"I talked to a prosecutor about this," he said. "Involving her would be a last resort tactic. It's risky and could benefit the defense. They'd play on the jury's sympathy for the poor woman. Any decent lawyer would advise her of her right not to testify against her family members."

"That's a shame," Brody said. "She could be the key to unraveling the whole thing. Find out what she knows, and the case is solved."

"Doesn't look like that's going to happen," he said. "At least not for now."

"Where is the car," I asked. "Where is the son hiding?"

"As far as I can tell no one has any idea," he said. "If they do they're keeping it quiet."

"Okay, thanks," I said. "I'll put these pictures in front of Tyler Scott. I'll let everyone know what he says as soon as I can."

I wasn't looking forward to another trek out into the wilderness to talk to the hermit, but I was committed. I was growing impatient with law enforcement too. How hard could the kid be to find? On the other hand, if they hadn't found him, there wasn't much point in Brody and me looking for him. We had nothing to go on. I had to trust that they were working some angle that I didn't know about.

We went back to the cabin so I could regroup. Brody loaded my backpack with necessities, including the now ever-present bear spray. I tucked the photos and my weapon inside with the bottles of water and snacks. I had the GPS, a flashlight, and just about anything I could need, just in case. I got a farewell kiss and drove back up the drive towards Tennessee.

I knew the way well enough by then, but when I arrived the hermit wasn't home. His camp was still intact, so I assumed he hadn't disappeared. I made myself at home and waited. He didn't return until almost dark. He had some goodies he'd looted from Beech Mountain.

"I would have thought you would lay low with all the heat on you," I said.

"A man's got to eat," he said. "This is what I do."

"I've got pictures for you to look at," I said, handing him the photos.

He sat down on a stump and thumbed through them, pausing on the picture of the car.

"That's the man, and that's the car," he said. "I'm fairly certain on the man. Still ninety-percent on the car. I think that's the one, but they all look alike these days."

"Do you know who this man is?"

"I do not," he said. "Told you before. I don't know anyone. Is he a bad guy?"

"He's the Chief of Police on Beech Mountain," I said.

"Well that changes things," he said. "What the hell is going on?"

I spent the time explaining to him what we thought had happened. I let him mull it over for several minutes. I hoped that he'd still be willing to testify. The average citizen may have second thoughts about testifying against law enforcement. I wasn't dealing with the average citizen.

"I know what I saw," he said. "I have no doubt that this is the man who carried that girl into the lake. The car is a dime a dozen around here, but I'd say it's just like the one I saw."

"When the time comes, will you testify to that effect?"

"I'd rather not involve myself," he said. "But I don't see where I have any choice."

"Let's get this straight," I said. "I want you to show up in court and help us, but you do have a choice. You have free will. You have freedom. I've done my best to help you maintain that freedom after you help us, but you can back out at any time."

"I think you know better than that," he said. "But I appreciate your efforts. Are you saying you have arranged a deal on my behalf?"

"The case has to come before the court first," I said. "Identifying the Chief is a big step in that direction."

"What is it that you're not telling me?"

"We don't think the Chief killed the girl," I said. "We think his son did. He was just hiding the evidence."

"I wouldn't know," he said. "She was dead when I first saw her. Didn't know if it was a girl or a boy, but it was the man in those pictures."

"One more thing," I said. "It's about your daughter."

"Good or bad?"

"She wants you to come home," I said. "Take it all back. Live in your house. Regain your previous life."

"A very nice sentiment," he said. "Never say never, but I don't think I can do that."

"Allow me to make a suggestion," I said. "Go see her. Give her a big hug and tell her you love her. Stay with her until the court proceedings are over. Then decide what to do next."

"I could clean up and get that business suit you were talking about," he said. "Is that what you want?"

"It's not about what I want," I said. "But you have a life back there if you want it. Otherwise stay out here. Makes no difference to me."

"It's going to require more thought," he said. "I appreciate you bringing me the message. I know you mean well. As far as this murder goes, come get me when you've got it all wrapped up. I'll point the man out in court. Tell them what I saw. That's all I can do, assuming I won't be arrested in the process."

"I'm paying a good lawyer to make sure that doesn't happen," I said. "No deal, no testimony. You've got my assurance on that."

"Your money?" he said. "Why would you do that? Couldn't you approach my daughter instead?"

"I've never met your daughter," I said. "I have met you. I'm happy to pay for you to retain your freedom. I'd also be happy for reimbursement if you decide to return to normal society, but it's not a requirement."

"You're an odd one, Breeze," he said. "At first I only thought you cared because you needed my help. I played along because I knew that I'd have to help if I could. Now I think maybe it's something more than that."

"Freedom," I said. "Do what you need to do. I'm doing my best to persuade you, but in the end, you've got to do what's best for you."

"I will," he said. "Not for you and not for my daughter. We'll see where it takes me, but I'll be ready when you are. After that, who knows?"

Nineteen

My hermit friend had positively identified the Beech Mountain Chief of Police as the person who'd put the girl's body in the lake. We thought maybe we'd found the crime scene. Two corners of the triangle had been taken care of. As soon as the car was found, the third and final corner would be filled in. Between the efforts of law enforcement and the work of Brody and me, we'd turned an impossible case into a solvable one. What happened that night on the mountain was slowly taking shape, but there were still questions to be answered.

We now had the leverage that we needed to pressure the Chief, maybe even charge him. He wouldn't be able to remain silent for long. He was an active participant in a murder. His trial would excite the local populace. His life in this area was over, no matter the outcome. The court would do everything within its power to determine the truth. That's what we all wanted after all.

Brody was waiting for me at the door when I got home. She let Red out so he could run to greet me.

"It's blood," she said. "No longer a mystery stain."

"How long before they can match the girl's DNA?"

"Twenty-four to seventy-two hours," she said.

"Any word on the car?"

"Not yet," she said. "At least not that I've heard."

"Tyler Scott saw the Chief that night," I said. "He's positive."

"Will he say so in court?"

"He says he will," I said. "But we can't be certain until he shows up when requested."

"We've got to tell the cops," she said. "They can get the ball rolling with the Chief. This might be the wedge we needed to make him talk."

"Fire up the SAT phone," I said. "I know it's important, but I don't feel like driving to Boone again. Seems like we live down there."

"Give me a minute," she said. "It's in the charger. I'll turn it on."

I threw a tennis ball for Red a few times, making sure to stop and pet him real good each time he brought it back. He was happy to see me. Dogs have short memories. He'd forgotten about how little attention I'd paid him recently. His tail wagged and his ears flopped like this was the greatest day of his life.

"I've got Rominger," Brody said. "I already told him, but he wants to talk to you."

She knew that I hated talking on the phone, even a secure one like this.

"Yo," I said.

"Is this hermit character a reliable witness?" he asked. "I'm going to the DA blind here."

"You mean will a homeless bum be believable in court?" I asked.

"Something like that," he said. "But also, will he show up?"

"I'm working on immunity for him," I explained. "I think he will appear, but I can't guarantee it. As far as court goes, if he cleans up first, he'll be an outstanding witness. He's sober and smart. Don't forget he was once a professional."

"That's what I was hoping to hear," he said. "I'll ask for their advice on what to do with the Chief. I'm going to have to assure them that we have a solid witness."

"I'm ninety-five percent certain he'll show up and do a fine job," I said. "Assuming he has immunity. Emphasize that to the DA."

"Will do," he said. "Oh, and thanks. Your contributions won't go unnoticed."

"Great, now when are you going to find that car?"

"Our guys have been pulling over white Subarus for days now," he said. "It's becoming a joke at HQ."

"Too bad the kid didn't take off in a bright yellow Hummer," I said.

"If he's been driving our roads, we would have found him by now," he said. "That's our thing. You know, Highway Patrol? He's got to be in deep hiding."

"Lots of hiding places in these mountains," I said. "But the kid isn't going it alone. Someone has to be hiding him."

"Maybe his father knows where he went," Rominger said. "We'll bring him in after I get legal advice. Charge him with something so we can hold him. That ought to break the dam on this thing. I'm starting to think we can get to the bottom of this, for the first time. I hate to admit it, but it's mostly because of you."

"And Brody, and Red," I said. "Creekside Investigations. What do you think?"

"Hanging a shingle?" he asked.

"I don't know," I said. "We mentioned the possibility. Brody has the background for it."

"And you've got some skills," he said. "Adding the dog to the mix gives you a formidable team."

"Thanks," I said. "That's kind of what we were thinking."

"If we get a murder conviction in this case," he said. "It would be a great jumpstart to your business."

"We'll worry about that later," I said. "Let's get this thing done first."

I rounded up Red and went inside. The kitchen smelled like something good to eat. My pretty woman was putting plates on the table. I stood inside the door feeling blessed. I'd never really experienced that feeling of gratitude. I'd had ups and downs. I'd been financially stable, and I'd been dead broke. I'd had a string of women come and go. At that moment, I realized that I was experiencing the best time of my life. I owed it all to Brody.

I gave her an unexpected hug and held it for an extra few seconds. I looked into her sparkly eyes and asked if she was as happy as I was.

"I am happy here," she said. "And I'm happy with you. You seem to have come to life here in the mountains. You've found your purpose."

"My purpose is to love you," I said. "This is spur of the moment, so I don't have a ring yet, but will you marry me? I promise you my undying love, for as long as we both shall live."

"I never imagined that you'd ask me that," she said.

I never imagined that I'd ask it," I admitted. "But right now I can't think of anything that I want more. Please, be my lawfully wedded wife."

"I will," she said. "You may now kiss the bride."

We kissed and hugged for a ridiculous amount of time, right there in the kitchen. Red joined us to see what the fuss was all about. We both knelt down to include him in the group hug. He gave each of us a big doggie kiss. No matter how long I live, or what happens to me in this life, I will never forget that moment. I'd finally shed all the demons within me. I'd finally realized what giving yourself completely to another person really meant. All of the bad memories that had haunted me for so long melted away. I had a future, and its name was Brody.

Our bedroom activities kept us up late into the night. All previous scorecards were forgotten. The slate had been wiped clean, and we expended enough energy in the process to light a small town. My sleep was deep and without dreams. When I woke, I was ready to face anything. The first thing I had to face was Red. We both slept too late, and he was impatient to go outside. He violated the bedroom boundary to put his nose in my face and remind me of my duties.

"Sorry, boy," I said. "I'm coming."

I let him out the back door and started the coffee maker. Before I could get my first cup, Angelina Will's car appeared in the driveway. She was the last person I cared to see that morning, but she wouldn't have come if it wasn't important. I quickly put on some pants and woke Brody.
"We've got company," I said. "I'll stall her while you get dressed."
"Her?"
"Yea, sorry," I said. "Something must be up."

I remembered that Red was outside and scrambled to call him in before Angelina got out of the car. I was too late. He had his muzzle in her face, accepting kisses and rubs. He was an equal opportunity lover.
"Good morning," I said. "You want some coffee?"
"I don't need to come inside," she said. "Be nice if you had a phone."
"What's up?"
"The car turned up near Elk River Falls," she said. "Just the car, not Zack."
"Has it been taken in for evidence collection?"
"Happening now," she said. "But the kid is still missing."
"And?"

"Can you go looking for him?" she asked. "Maybe take your dog? We can get him a good scent off the car."

"A boat bum's work is never done," I said. "Why not canvas the area with your people? How far could he have gone?"

"Have you been there?" she asked. "Not exactly a walk in the park."

"We've been there," I said. "But not past the falls. I'd guess it's rough territory. Not the kind our boy would try to navigate."

"That's the issue, exactly," she said. "You're probably looking for a body at this point."

"Ah, fuck," I said. "You think he offed himself?"

"He's not camping out in the wilderness," she said. "It's a dangerous area."

"Where is the car now?" I asked. "Red needs a fresh scent and a trail to follow."

"It's where we found it," she said. "Until you can get there. Once you get what you need we'll haul it in for analysis."

"So, you mean, like now."

"Yea, sorry," she said. "Time is of the essence."

"We haven't even had breakfast," I said. "Not even Red."

"Do what you need to do to get ready," she said. "The car is just before the actual parking area at the falls. Off to the left and out of the way, like he didn't want to take up a parking spot that the hikers might need."

"Considerate of him," I said. "We've got to eat and take a shower. I need two hours. Don't let anyone near that car."

"Our department will reimburse you for your time," she said. "We don't have a dog."

"We'll help either way," I said. "Just bad timing is all."

"Long night?"

"I proposed to Brody," I said. "We celebrated."

"Congratulations, Breeze and Brody," she said. "See you at Elk River Falls in two hours."

First I had a dog's nose up in my face, then I had a femme fatale up in my face. I still wasn't fully awake but the day had been laid out for me. Me and Red were going to look for a body along the Elk River. Not exactly what I had planned. I didn't know if the Chief had been arrested. Angelina hadn't said. I'd let her get away without asking because I'd been off guard. I started thinking about moving somewhere else and regaining our anonymity, instead of opening a private detective business. Meanwhile, I had a job to do. If Zack was out there, Red would find him.

"You want to go hiking at Elk River Falls?" I asked Brody. "The car turned up there, but the kid didn't."

"That doesn't sound good," she said. "I'll go with you."

"I told her two hours," I said. "So we can eat and prepare properly. If we're looking for his body, it will keep that long."

"Is that what she thinks?" Brody asked. "That he's dead?"

"She certainly hinted at it," I said. "Remember when we hiked to those falls? All the warning signs about how dangerous it was."

"Yes," she said. "Kind of creeped me out at the time."

"If he went off the top of the falls, all we have to do is follow the river downstream," I said. "He'll get hung up in the rocks or the trees somewhere. Can't be far."

"Why couldn't the cops do that?"

"I suppose they are holding out hope that he's still alive, and that Red can find him."

"What's going on with the Chief?" she asked.

"Didn't think to ask," I said. "I wasn't fully awake at the time."

"Start the coffee," she said. "I'll start the bacon."

We finished breakfast and prepared a day pack for hiking. Red got excited when I opened the car's rear hatch and told him to get in. He hadn't been away from the cabin in a long time. It would be good for him to get out and follow a trail again. He seemed to live for the opportunity.

Police cruisers from several agencies lined the dirt road leading to the falls. I stopped when I saw Angelina. She directed Red and me to the Subaru. A gloved hand opened the driver's door, and I motioned for Red to pick up a scent. There was a light jacket in the backseat. I held it for Red to sniff. Within a few seconds, he let me know he was ready to hunt.

I kept him on the leash as we walked down the road towards the falls. He was clearly on Zack's trail, which continued in an obvious direction. Brody jogged to catch up.

"I've got a cop radio," she said. "No cell coverage out here."

The dirt road led to a well-worn but narrow trail. Red wanted to go faster, but I held him in check. He was confident he was going to find what we were looking for. He led us to the top of the falls and tried to go out onto the dangerous rocks that overlooked the river below. That was the end of the trail as far as he was concerned. It looked like our fears were about to be realized. I had Red search all around us, including at the base of the falls and alongside the river, but he never picked up the scent again.

The Elk River was flowing at a moderate rate. Water depth ranged from a few inches to three or four feet deep. Boulders were strewn everywhere. I studied the current and depth for a minute, trying to decide if a body could make it downstream at all. I decided that it was possible. A living person would get beat all to hell on the rocks, but a limp, freshly dead body could slither and bounce through them, at least for a while.

The river wound its way back towards Banner Elk from here. The only thing we could do was follow it.
"Look for rocks where we can get out in the river and look downstream," I told Brody. "Also take note of any place where we can cross, in case he's washed up on the other side."
"Gotcha," she said. "Let's roll."

Red wasn't pleased that the target had not been found, but he was happy to be in the woods with us. He gave a doggie shrug and followed along, tail wagging. Parts of the walk were easy, but the farther we got from the falls, the denser the forest became. Several times we had to leave the river's edge to find an easier path. Each time we returned to the banks, we'd take several minutes to search the water for any sign of Zack. I saw more than one spot that looked as if a body couldn't pass through, but we continued searching.

We took a break for water and rest. I tried to give Red a drink, but he preferred the river water. Brody and I sat on the rocks and contemplated our efforts.
"Nice day for a walk in the woods," she said. "But how long do we keep this up?"
"He's got to be near here," I said. "The water is getting thinner. We'll find him soon."

I was right about that. Zack's body was less than a half-mile from where we'd rested. It was, however, on the opposite side of the river. A combination of rocks and fallen trees snagged him, stopping his progress. We had to backtrack a bit to a safe crossing point. Then we had to get wet to free the corpse and drag it onto dry land. He had obvious trauma to the head.

We used the radio to call Angelina, and the GPS to give her coordinates. We explained the terrain and left the recovery decisions up to her. There was a pause before she responded.
"Can a chopper get to him?" she asked.
"No place to land," I said. "But they could lower a basket. Trees are thirty, maybe forty feet tall."

"Stand by," she said.

Red sniffed the body while we waited. He looked up at me and cocked his head sideways.

"That's him, boy," I said. "You found him. Good boy." That satisfied him. I got a treat out of my pack and rewarded him. He carried it away from the body before eating it.

"What do you think went on here?" Brody asked. "Why did he kill himself?"

"He must have thought it preferable to going to jail for the rest of his life," I said.

"First he ran, and now this," she said. "We can't bring him to trial, but the case appears to be solved."

"A rather unsatisfying ending," I said. "If it is indeed the end."

"Why wouldn't it be?"

"The cops still have the Chief to deal with," I said. "What if the son was protecting the father, instead of the other way around?"

"What father would let his son take the rap like that?" she asked. "Highly improbable."

"Maybe there's more to this than we know," I said. "Then again, maybe it's exactly what it appears to be."

"Don't tell me," she said. "Your gut is questioning our conclusions."

"I can't quite put my finger on it," I said. "We've done a good job unraveling this thing, damn good job actually, but I keep worrying that we've missed something."

"Because of those dreams?"

"I've tried to dismiss them as just dreams," I said. "You and I have turned this thing inside out. Maybe my lack of investigative experience makes me question my findings. When you think about it, this hasn't been that difficult. Too easy is what I'm thinking."

"Occam's Razor," she said. "The simplest solutions are more likely to be correct than the complex ones."

"I shouldn't make more assumptions than the minimum needed," I said.

"I haven't heard it put that way before," she said. "I don't agree with the way you framed it. We shouldn't assume anything. We should be guided by the facts, which all lead to Zack as the murderer."

"I can't disagree with you," I said. "Just keep an open mind. If alternatives present themselves, we should look into them."

"He's dead," she said. "We can't ask him if he did it."

"His mother has apparently been committed," I said. "That only leaves the Chief."

"We'll have to see how this development affects him," she said. "No point in protecting his son now."

"True," I said. "There's no reason he shouldn't talk. He's still facing charges of some kind. He can probably buy some leniency if he tells the whole story."

The body was lifted out of the woods and Brody, and I were left to hike back to our car. Red was having a grand time roaming about. I'd let him off the leash after the chopper left. We'd done our job, it was time for him to have a little fun. When we reached the dirt road, everyone was gone but Angelina. The Subaru was gone too.

"Thank you for this," she said. "Avery County will be cutting you a check for your time."

"Sorry about how it worked out," I said. "But it's what we all expected."

"What's going on with the Chief?" Brody asked Angelina.

"He's in custody," she said. "I don't know the details yet."

"Who took him in?" I asked.

"Highway Patrol," she said. "They've been working with the DA's office. I'm just shoe leather."

"As are we," I told her. "I'd be curious to know how that works out. We've invested a lot of time in this."

"I'll talk to Rominger," she said. "He can fill you in if and when it's appropriate."

"I appreciate it," I said. "I guess we're finished here."
"Do you mind if I say goodbye to Red?" she asked.

I looked to Brody before responding. She gave me a shrug.
"No problem," I said.
She knelt and petted him. He responded with a big wet kiss. He didn't know or care about our human tensions. He was an equal opportunity licker. Angelina stood and gave me a nod. I took it as our final farewell, which suited me just fine. Then she turned to Brody and did the same. I took that as a sign of respect.

We loaded Red in the car and drove out of there. We'd accomplished what we came to do, but we still felt let down. The excitement of the chase was over. There was nothing left for us to do. We'd worked hard and made some personal sacrifices to assist law enforcement. Now it was in their hands. We had to depend on them, and the legal system, to finish out the mission. Brody had plenty of experience with that, but I did not. I hated waiting on other people or depending on them, but I had no standing going forward. I wasn't a cop, a lawyer, or a judge. I was a simple boat bum turned mountain man. Other than producing the hermit, my part was done.

Twenty

Two days passed before we heard the first word about what was going on. The waiting, and the not knowing, was driving both of us crazy. I was relieved to see Rominger coming down the driveway. Finally, we'd learn something.

"Long story," he said. "You got a minute?"

"We're all ears," I said. "I'll put some coffee on."

"Miss Brody," he said, taking his hat off as he came inside.

"Good to see you, Rominger," she said. "You're the closest thing we have to a friend up here. You're always welcome in our home."

"I'll get right to it," he said. "It looks like you're going to have to bring the hermit to court."

"The Chief's still not talking?" I asked.

"Not really," he said. "Only through his lawyer. He indicates that he will plead not guilty to any charges we can bring."

"What's his strategy?" I asked. "His son is dead and gone. Why not give it up?"

"I'm just the bearer of news," he said. "I'm no lawyer, but he's got an expensive one. If you ask me, I think he's banking on the hermit's testimony being a bust."

"If he can't be put at the scene, could he skate?" I asked.

"Your friend Tyler Scott is the only one that can connect him to this entire mess," he said. "If he doesn't show, the Chief walks. If the defense can tear apart the witness, he also stands a chance of getting off. At this point, a jury may show sympathy due to the death of his son. Everyone assumes the son is the killer. Why punish the father? I think his strategy is sound."

"But he covered it up," I said. "He disposed of the body. He's a law enforcement officer. He's supposed to be on the side of justice."

"I'm sure you've thought of this," he said. "But a jury is going to give him a lot of leeway. Half the potential juror pool would protect their own offspring."

"They might if it was them," I said. "But they'll hold a cop to a higher standard."

"He's still human," he said. "One who's lost his kid and whose wife is in the nut hut."

"A very sympathetic character," Brody said. "But the truth is still the truth."

"I'm not a lawyer, like I told you," he said. "But the hermit had better be damn good, or the Chief will go free. That's my take on it. That's what the Chief's counsel is depending on."

"Innocent until proven guilty," Brody said. "Plus reasonable doubt. Basic American legal standards."

"Meanwhile, the car is positive for the girl's DNA," Rominger said. "So is the blood at the resort. We've got serious evidence against somebody in the Chief's family. One of them killed the girl. Of that, there is no doubt."

"Which seriously hurts the defense case," I said. "The Chief is holding onto a very fine thread."

"He doesn't have to prove his son's innocence," he said. "Only his own. Without the hermit, he can't be tied to any of it."

"I get it," Brody said. "His only crime is dumping the body. That's the only way he participated. If we can't prove that, then he's home free."

"Correct," Rominger said. "Therefore, you are back on the payroll. Bringing the witness to court is of the utmost importance. I should add that bringing him in Daniel Boone clothes won't be a lot of help. We don't need a mail bomber look-alike as our star witness."

"I need to follow up on his immunity first," I said. "Then I'll need a court date."

"The wheels of justice turn slowly," he said. "An actual court appearance could be months away. Depending on how hard the defense drags its heels."

"His lawyer is Joshua Dorman," I said. "Find out how that negotiation is going. Put some pressure on somebody. It's important that your witness won't feel threatened."

"The warrants were pursued by the Chief," he said. "A clear conflict of interest. I don't think it's going to be a problem. There is no movement on Beech Mountain to have the hermit arrested."

"He won't assume safe passage until he has it in writing," I said. "His freedom is very important to him. He's a pretty sharp guy. He's not the image you have in your mind."

"He is still a small-time thief," he said. "Romanticize him all you want."

"He knows that," I said. "That's why we need the immunity."

"Does it come with a promise to cease his activities?"

"No, it does not," I said. "But I can't speak for him. I can only relay messages."

"I'm sure the DA will let him slide in exchange for his testimony," he said. "The Chief is a much bigger fish."

"That's what we're counting on," I said. "Exert whatever influence you have."

"That's his lawyer's responsibility," he said. "But I'll put in a good word."

"We'll go speak to the lawyer later today," I said. "Thanks for the update."

By the time we made it to Dorman's office, there had been further developments. The Chief was being charged with accessory liability. The charge claimed that after the fact, the Chief assisted the offender in order to prevent his apprehension. It carried a sentence of up to fifteen years in prison. Various obstruction charges were tacked on for good measure, but would likely be dropped if the defendant accepted a plea deal.

No one wanted to worry about the hermit's petty crimes, only that he testify. He would be granted immunity. I had to not only get the word to Tyler Scott, but also bring him in to speak with his lawyer and the District Attorney's Office. If the case went to trial, he'd have to return to civilization yet again. It all rested on his appearance and credible testimony. There was still no other solid evidence tying the Chief to the crime.

"Without a murder trial for the son," Dorman said. "The case against the Chief rests entirely with Tyler Scott. Without him, it all falls apart. All the well-founded suspicions in the world won't put the father behind bars."

"I'll do my best to bring him in," I said. "But understand, it's not up to me. Scott has to do this willingly. You can subpoena him if you want, but good luck finding him."

"If we did subpoena him and he failed to appear, would you lead law enforcement to him?"

"I would not," I said. "I promised that the decision was his and his alone. It seemed to persuade him to cooperate."

"Interesting dilemma," he said. "What if the court compelled you to cooperate?"

"Do you mean to force me to reveal his location?" I asked.

"Hypothetically," he said.

"I suspect they'd have an equally hard time finding me," I said. "I've been the driving force behind solving this case. I've not only cooperated, I've volunteered my time and resources. I'm not an enemy of the court, and I won't allow that characterization to stand."

"Easy now, Breeze," he said. "I was only theorizing. I'm sure they appreciate your contributions. It's just that they'll be frustrated as hell if the hermit fails to produce."

"Let's just say that I'm aware of his importance," I said. "I'll do my best. That's all I can do."

"A lot of people are depending on you," he said. "And a mysterious hermit."

I didn't like what I felt when I left the lawyer's office. Maybe I overreacted, but the idea of somehow holding me legally accountable pissed me off. They would have had no case at all without me. They wouldn't even know about the son. I was the one who'd discovered the hermit and tracked him down. Brody, Red, and I were the only successful investigators to work the case. I was close to telling them to shove it up their ass, but Brody calmed me down.

"He was only kicking ideas around," she said. "He wasn't speaking for the DA's office or the cops."

"It was ill-thought out," I said. "But he doesn't know me. He should have guessed how I would react."

"He couldn't know," she said. "He's okay. Don't hold it against him. He's a lawyer, all caught up in the higher echelon of polite society. He's got no idea what you're all about."

"You're right," I said. "Thanks. Always the reasonable one."

"It's a two-way street," she said. "I have benefited greatly from your appreciation of freedom and your non-conforming lifestyle."

"If what that lawyer suggested comes to pass," I said. "We might be living out there with the hermit."

"I don't want that for us," she said. "But I'll go anywhere with you."

"Don't worry," I said. "I think my wilderness friend will appear. I'll go find him tomorrow."

"You want me to go with you?"

"I would, but it's best I go alone," I said. "I don't want to do anything to spook him. Hell, I hope he's still there."

There was an underlying tension in the house that night. It wasn't between Brody and me. It involved that slightest suggestion that I'd want to cut and run if pressed by a court. It also involved the possibility that the hermit would ultimately decide not to cooperate. I gave the chance of his refusal only ten percent odds, but it was enough to keep me feeling uneasy. I didn't do a lot to prepare for another walk in the wilderness. I didn't need stealth or even a weapon. I knew the way well enough by now. I took a few shots of Tennessee Whisky before going to bed, just to take the edge off.

In the morning I walked Red while Brody cooked breakfast. For some reason, I wasn't particularly enthused about the day's mission. All the mystery surrounding the hermit was gone. He was a man, made of flesh and blood like everyone else. He survived more on thievery than on wilderness skills. He even had his old life to fall back on if necessary. I had to give him credit for resisting that urge. I was certain that his meager existence involved plenty of hardships, but he had his freedom. I would do nothing to interfere with that.

It was mid-morning before I made the drive into Tennessee. I was deep into the wild before noon. I made good time due to my lack of caution. I did not worry about danger or announcing my presence. I didn't need to remain silent or sneak through the forest. I didn't stop to appreciate nature or take in the sights and sounds of the mountain. I took a direct and purposeful course to the hermit's lair. I crawled through the tunnel, stopping at the curtain blocking the inner sanctum.
"It's Breeze," I said. "Coming in."

There was no response. After I stood up in the clearing, I could see that he wasn't there. I took a quick look around. All his stuff was still there. Inside the tent, I found a note written in big letters on a piece of cardboard.
At my daughter's house in Linville Ridge.

That's all it said. It was really his house, but he'd referred to it as his daughter's. Had he given up his hermit life? I didn't even know where this house was. I'd have to get the address from Rominger. Fuck. I'd walked out here for nothing. Those small tensions would stay with me until I talked with Tyler Scott.

I took down the note and crawled back out, miffed that I'd wasted my time. On the way back it occurred to me that this could be a good thing. Maybe it meant that he was on board with the court proceedings. It would be a lot more convenient to be in Banner Elk instead of out in the wilderness. He could stay comfortably with his daughter and participate fully in the prosecution of the Chief.

That thought appeased my anger. I kept an eye out for bears and marched back to the car. I drove back into North Carolina, through Banner Elk, and home to Brody. I handed her the note as soon as I walked in.
"Long hike for nothing," I said.
"Do we even know his daughter's name?" she asked.
"No name, no address," I said. "We'll have to ask the cops."
"Reason four zillion why we need a cellphone," she said.

"A conversation for another time," I said. "You want to ride down to Boone for the four zillionth time?"
"I'm sure Miss Will can provide us with the information," she said.

This was a trap. It was like a trick question. Did I want to see her again? If I didn't, did that mean I was still tempted by her? If I did, did that mean I was still attracted to her? There was no correct answer. Brody had effectively painted me into a corner, just like that. It was a subtle reminder that I came a little too close to screwing up. Then she let me off the hook.
"Just as easy to drive to Boone," she said.
"Boone it is," I said.

The daughter's name was Mary. After she'd divorced, she reclaimed her maiden name, Mary Scott. All I could think of was Mary Queen of Scots. By all appearances, she'd been reluctant to assume her father's wealth, but she had no choice. She couldn't leave his vacant house to rot, or his investments to go unattended. She'd reluctantly assumed her birthright, only moving in after the declaration of death was final. Now, dad was miraculously alive.

Rominger made a few calls on our behalf. Linville Ridge was a gated community. They didn't let any riff-raff off the street through the gates. Once we got the assurance that we'd be allowed to pass, we left Boone and headed to the house of Mary Scott.

Twenty-One

Mary answered the door, and we exchanged greetings. She led us into her living room. A well-groomed gentleman sat on the sofa, doing a crossword puzzle.

"You have friends here to see you, dad," Mary said.

I had not recognized Tyler Scott, even though I knew he was here. He was wearing nice clothes and had obviously been to a barber. His attire was top of the line stuff. He had new leather loafers on his feet. He didn't resemble the hermit in the least.

"Is that you?" I asked. "Quite the transformation."

"I wanted to make a nice appearance for the lawyers and judges," he said. "You told me that this would add weight to what I had to say."

"I'm certain it will," I said. "You've heard the recent developments?"

"Actually, no," he said. "I'm still shunning some modern conveniences, like TV for example."

"We don't watch it," I told him. "No cell phone either."

"Where do we stand with the case?"

"The son, whom we assume is the killer, is dead," I said. "Apparent suicide. His car is positive for the victim's DNA. The father, who you saw dump the body, is still not talking. His hopes rest on you not testifying, or not being credible."

"I'm fully prepared to cooperate," he said. "What about my deal?"

"You have immunity," I said. "No one is going to arrest you."

"Someone will contact me with the time and place?"

"First you need to go to Boone and talk to your lawyer," I said. "Some paperwork to sign. Then the DA will want to question you. They need to know what you know before court."

"Perfectly understandable," he said. "A chance for me to do my civic duty."

"That's one way to look at it," I said. "If it's okay, I'll give the phone number here to your lawyer."

"Let me give you my cell," Mary said. "That's the best way to contact us."

She wrote her number on a post-it note and handed it to me. I gave it to Brody. Three of us were still standing while the ex-hermit sat. It felt awkward.

"I should thank you," Mary said. "Because of you dad has come to visit. I've been waiting for him to come home for a long time."

"Will you be sticking around, Tyler?" I asked.

"That remains to be seen," he said. "I'm here for a purpose. Once that's done I'll have to make some choices."

"We'll get out of your hair," I said. "I'm sure you'll do fine with the lawyers."

I was happy to learn that Tyler Scott intended to testify. I was amazed at his transformation, but he'd been cool to our presence. I don't know what I'd expected, but it was like he wasn't the same man. Coming in out of the wilderness had instantly changed him back into the man he used to be, the one he'd left behind. I couldn't square it in my head.

We drove to Boone to give his lawyer Mary's cell number. He'd already been given her house phone number by Rominger. The entirety of the local judiciary and law enforcement waited on the word of a hermit. What they'd get is the word of a businessman. It didn't bode well for the Chief.

We left the lawyer's office and went to see Rominger. All I wanted was an assurance that we'd be kept in the loop. He made it clear that we would know everything that happened, as soon as he knew.

"Depending on how the early hearings go, they might need you to testify," he said.

"To what?" I asked. "The case seems pretty clear."

"It could get complicated," he said. "How did we find out the son was in that house? How did we locate the hermit? That kind of stuff."

"I'll do it if I have to," I said. "But a courtroom is the last place I want to be."

"The DA will have all the leverage once he talks to our star witness," he said. "Probably won't ever get to court. The Chief is screwed."

"I feel a little bad for him," I said. "His son is dead, and his wife is locked away. He won't ever be a cop again. His life is over."

"His choices," Rominger said. "Nothing we can do about it."

Wherever you find yourself in life, it is the product of your choices, I understood that all too well. I'd made more than my share of bad decisions. Some were under duress, but some were because I'd been stupid. I knew right from wrong quite clearly, but that didn't mean I'd also chosen the right thing to do. That is the nature of humanity I guess. I can make no excuses for my bad choices. I made them freely, knowing the potential consequences. So had the Chief.

My work on this case had brought him down. Tyler Scott's testimony would put the last nail in his coffin. I was responsible for that too. The weight of that responsibility landed suddenly on my shoulders. Brody hadn't spoken since we'd left Joshua Dorman's office.
"I'd be interested in your thoughts," I said.
"I agree with your sympathy for the Chief," she said. "Have we got this right?"
"The one thing we are certain of is that he dropped the body in the lake," I said. "That's the bedrock of this entire case."
"He had his reasons," she said. "Reasons that many parents would agree with."
"His lawyer will need to convince someone on the jury to agree," I said. "He'll get his day in court, if he so chooses."
"Yes, but they didn't charge him with murder or even being an accomplice," she said. "He's guilty of accessory after the fact. Guilty as hell."
"Seems that way," I said. "We have to let the court do its duty. Blind justice and all that."
"The next time you agree to work a case, make sure we get to celebrate when it's over."

"Creekside Investigations," I said. "We won't take a case we can't celebrate."

"Think it will fit on a business card?"

We went home and awaited word on the legal proceedings. Our life returned to normal. I got to spend plenty of time with Red, and his attitude improved greatly. We took long walks up the mountain most every day. Brody started a rug hooking project. We sat each night in front of the fire, reading and forgetting about the outside world. It was a peaceful existence, the one we'd come here to find.

Soon enough we got a visit from Rominger. We welcomed him in, eager to hear some news.

"Who was that guy you sent in place of the hermit?" he asked.

"That's Tyler Scott," I said. "VP and CFO of a bank."

"No shit," he said. "Everyone was deeply impressed by him, except the Chief's lawyers, of course."

"What happened?"

We all sat down at the kitchen table. Brody poured the coffee. Red came in to see what all the fuss was about. Rominger laid it out for us.

"Tyler Scott was more than credible," he said. "He was composed and thoughtful. He walked the DA through the entire chain of events with a clarity of thought and recall. He was unimpeachable. The defense shit a brick and ran to beg the Chief to take a deal."

"Did he plea?"

"Wait," he said. "I haven't got to the good part. It didn't go down like any of us thought."

"What?" I asked. "What are you talking about?"

"The son didn't kill the girl," he said. "At least according to the father. None of us saw it coming, but he finally gave up and told us the story, as best he knew it."

"I'm not following," Brody said. "As best he knew it?"

"He only knows what the son told him," Rominger said. "It's all third party hearsay as far as the court is concerned."

"What did the son tell him?" I asked.

"Here's the kicker," he began. "The mother did it. Blew us all out of the water."

"The son blamed the mom?" Brody asked.

"Swore to his dad," he said. "He met the girl at the ski resort. His mother had dropped him off. She was to pick him up at a certain time. The girl had a little weed. She walked with him to the parking lot and they stopped in the shadows to smoke a joint, but the mom sees them. She freaks out and confronts the pair. The girl doesn't back down, gives the mom some lip. Lighten up you old hag. Mom explodes in a fit of rage and bashes the girl to the ground, picks up a rock and whacks her in the head. Blood everywhere. Then the mother zones out, leaving the son to deal with the aftermath. Turns out she has a long history of these sort of episodes. Spent several stints at Broughton Hospital in Morgantown. Schizophrenic, manic depressive, whatever. The son gets her in the car, picks up the girl and puts her in the back, then drops it all on daddy's lap."

"Holy shit," I said. "The experience drove him to suicide."

"I hate to say it," he said. "But it was the best way to spare both his parents."

"How so?"

"He's the only witness to the murder," he said. "Nothing he told his father can be used in court. The mother can't be compelled to testify. All she has to do is remain crazy, which apparently isn't a charade. The Chief is left holding the bag, but there is a lot of sympathy for him in the aftermath of this."

"We were thinking the same thing," I said. "But we have to remember that he hindered the investigation. He dropped the girl in the lake. Without the hermit, we'd have never known."

"The DA is inclined to show leniency," he said. "A judge may think differently. He was an officer of the law and subject to a higher standard. I can't say how it will play out from here."

"I'm glad it's not my decision to make," I said.

"Me too."

"Me three," Brody added.

A few days passed before I decided to visit Tyler Scott at his daughter's place. The security guard called her, and she granted us permission to enter the gated community. She answered the door with tears in her eyes.

"He's gone," she said. "Left in the middle of the night. Left a note telling me he loved me, but not to look for him."

"I'm sorry, ma'am," I said. "Truly sorry."

"Can you find him again?" she asked. "I can't live here in peace knowing that he's cold and hungry. I feel so guilty. I just need a chance to help him understand."

"I can't make him come back," I said. "I'd like to thank him myself, but he's chosen freedom. I have to respect that."

"Please," she said. "Go talk to him. At least try."

It was clear to me that she was sincere. He'd given her everything that any person could have wanted, but she wanted him. She wanted her father to be there for her. She wanted him to appreciate his wealth, share it with him. I believed her.

"I'll give it an honest try," I said. "I'll relay your message, that's all I can do."

"Thank you, Breeze," she said. "Thanks for everything."

I left the next day for Tennessee, and the stretch of wilderness Tyler Scott called home. He'd done his duty, now he'd returned to the life he truly wanted to live. I wouldn't try to convince him otherwise, but I did want to thank him. I'd tell him what his daughter said as well. The hike was quick and easy. I could do it blindfolded by now. I called for him before entering his camp, but he didn't respond.

I crawled through the brush and came into the opening that used to be his homestead. It was all gone. Everything was gone, except for a Brooks Brothers suit hanging on a tree limb. Fine Italian leather shoes were on the ground underneath. There was no note. I would not pursue him any further.

"Freedom, brother," I said to the woods. "Be free, and be happy."

Author's Thoughts

In previous books, I mentioned the State Police. The proper name for this agency is the North Carolina Highway Patrol. Thanks to the reader who corrected me.

All of the law enforcement agencies in this book are staffed with men and woman of high character. This is a work of fiction. I have no ill-will for any of the departments mentioned.

Buckeye Lake on Beech Mountain was actually drained of water in December 2018. The diver involved in the accident was rescued. There was no body found in the mud.

Joshua Dorman is a reader who contacted me about being a character in one of my books. I couldn't see how Breeze would cross paths with a lab manager from Massachusetts, so I made him a lawyer in Boone, North Carolina.

Angelina Will and I have mutual friends, but we've never met in person. My thanks to her for allowing me to use her name. Facebook is good for some things.

If you'd like to have a character named after you, or suggest ideas for future plots, feel free to contact me at: *Kimandedrobinson@gmail.com*

If you enjoyed this book, please leave a review at Amazon.com. Reviews are greatly appreciated.

It truly seems that half the cars on the road in western North Carolina are Subarus, most of them white.

Other Books in this Series

Banner Elk Breeze
https://amzn.to/2CHJM85

Blue Ridge Breeze
https://amzn.to/2sM4kaV

More Mountain Breeze Adventures Coming Soon

Ed Robinson's Previous Works also Starring Breeze

Trawler Trash
https://amzn.to/2UjXYeN

Following Breeze
https://amzn.to/2fXJgq2

Free Breeze
https://amzn.to/2fXILfv

Redeeming Breeze
https://amzn.to/2gbBjAx

Bahama Breeze
https://amzn.to/2fJiMe6

Cool Breeze
https://amzn.to/2weKg1l

True Breeze
https://amzn.to/2ws6Hzp

Ominous Breeze
https://amzn.to/2lPzg70

Restless Breeze
https://amzn.to/2Aicj0A

Enduring Breeze
https://amzn.to/2unav5I

Benevolent Breeze
https://amzn.to/2NCRA3f

Nonfiction by Ed Robinson

Leap of Faith; Quit Your Job and Live on a Boat
https://amzn.to/2G0z7bL

Poop, Booze, and Bikinis
https://amzn.to/2ThbW0M

The Untold Story of Kim
https://amzn.to/2WgLMx2

Acknowledgements

Proofreaders:
Dave Calhoun
Laura Spink (and Breeze the Golden)
Jeanene Olson
Rich Smail

Editor:
John Corbin

Cover Design:
Emily Brandz

Interior Formatting:
Rachael Cox

My thanks to all the contributors who helped turn this book into a quality product.

Made in the USA
Middletown, DE
14 July 2025